the Imperfect
Perfectionist

seasonal secrets for a happy, balanced life

written by
Michelle Babb
Wendy Lomme
Karen Pfeiffer Bush
Chieko Watanabe

Published by the Staggering Quills LLC, Seattle WA
www.theimperfectperfectionist.com

ISBN-13: 978-1499547863
ISBN-10: 1499547862

This book is dedicated to all of the hardworking, ultra-driven, multitasking, over-committed, sleep-deprived women who are ready to say ENOUGH IS ENOUGH! We hereby give you permission to abandon the internal struggle and we welcome you into our clan of recovering perfectionists.

Contents

Meet the Authors

Chieko Watanabe,
Business and Life Coach

 It was during kindergarten recess that Chieko stumbled across the art of coaching. One day, her friend Gretchen came to her with a seemingly unsolvable problem. Gretchen was the proud owner of She-Ra: Princess of Power action figure, which she loved. But, to have a meaningful collection, she desperately wanted the He-man action figure to play with, but she was afraid that He-man was only for boys. Racking her six-year-old brain, Chieko helped her friend come up with a strategy and drum up the courage needed to ask for He-man from her mom.

Chieko continues to help people achieve their dreams and live their best lives. She is a coach, an author, and a keynote speaker devoted to empowering her clients to take charge of their businesses and their lives. She is the founder of Dominate Your Business and loves nothing more than helping people build confidence and create an amazing life.

Chieko's favorite tidbits from *The Imperfect Perfectionist*:

- Michelle's delicious recommendations inspire me to try new foods and recipes, including roasted Brussels sprouts, which are now my new favorite!
- I adore Karen's story of her flying pigs client and now only fill my home with things that warm my heart.
- I have a whole new appreciation for enjoying the rain thanks to Wendy's fearless embrace of all things nature.

Michelle Babb, MS, RD, Nutritionist

Michelle might have been described as a picky eater when she was a child. Her diet consisted mostly of mac n' cheese and fish and chips. Michelle's favorite breakfast was "Caramel Breakfast Ring," made with canned biscuit dough and brown sugar and cooked in the microwave until properly gooey. She openly rejected most of the veggies that her mom served up (mainly because they were canned or part of a TV dinner) but happily munched on fresh carrots, radishes, and peas plucked straight from her grandma's garden.

Michelle honored her preference for fresh, local, whole foods when she decided to pursue a master's degree in nutrition from Bastyr University and then became a registered dietitian. Michelle has a private practice in West Seattle, where she specializes in mind-body nutrition, weight management, and inflammatory digestive disorders. She is the author of *Anti-Inflammatory Eating Made Easy* and teaches nutrition-themed cooking classes at Puget Consumers Co-op (PCC). Michelle's passion for intelligent, intuitive eating is infectious and will change your relationship with food forever.

Michelle's favorite tidbits from *The Imperfect Perfectionist*:

- Chieko's advice to take care of tolerations allowed me to finally part with my three-gallon jug of stinky lotion, which now belongs to Wendy.
- Karen encouraged me to find and claim a Peace Zone in my bedroom, where I now am inspired to do most of my writing.
- Thanks to Wendy's suggestion to extend your living space outdoors, I did some serious remodeling of my rooftop deck and am savoring Seattle summers from my outdoor living room.

Karen Pfeiffer Bush, Professional Organizer and Home Stager

Karen's parents would tell you that her bedroom was often a disaster zone when she was a child. But if you looked closely, you would discover that Karen emptied her closet to set up an office with a typewriter, an adding machine, and a Rolodex, as every eight-year-old girl needs. This was her very first Peace Zone and office to organize to her heart's content. While playing "business," Karen got an early start honing her organizational skills.

Fast-forward to 2014: Karen is a professional organizer, certified relocation specialist, writer, speaker, and founder of LifeSpace: Home Organization and Transition Support as well as Housewarming Home Staging and Design. Fear not! She can help ANYONE create a beautiful AND functional home. Karen's unique "funorganizing" tips will help bring more happiness and fun into your home all year-round.

Karen's favorite tidbits from *The Imperfect Perfectionist*:

- Michelle's food prep tips inspired me to always be prepared with healthy food options for my family.
- Wendy's plant-snipping tips motivated me to bring the outside in.
- Chieko's advice adjusted my thinking in setting intentions instead of focusing on goals.

Wendy Lomme, Landscape Designer

Wendy's love for the outdoors was led by her cat, Scooter. Tromping the twenty acres on her home in New England, eight-year-old Wendy loved nothing more than to follow her adventurous kitty around the grounds. The two would strut down to the stream, around the edge of the pool, up to the tree fort, and behind the barn, where Scooter would get high on the catnip and roll down the hill with Wendy in tow.

Today, Wendy is the proud owner of Akina Designs, a landscaping company dedicated to beautifying the outdoors while creating healthy, happy environments for families, pets, communities, and the earth alike. She'll help you discover your green thumb and inspire you to eagerly embrace outdoor experiences, rain or shine.

Wendy's favorite tidbits from *The Imperfect Perfectionist*:

- The pocket full of beets story from Michelle inspired me to give radishes another try.
- Using a timer as Karen suggested made overwhelming tasks disappear in a matter of minutes.
- I learned from Chieko to zap my tolerations, and now I get to spend more time with my friends and family.

Introduction
Seasoned Advice from Four Perfectly Imperfect Women

Perfectionism. That all-too-familiar feeling that anything less than flawless is a failure. As perfectionists, we've always colored inside the lines, made the honor roll, been the star athletes, and excelled in the workplace. We hold ourselves to the highest possible standards—our own. While being a perfectionist definitely has its merits, it can also rob us of our time, prevent us from taking chances, and leave us feeling woefully inadequate when things don't turn out exactly as planned. Not to mention that being perfect is exhausting!

As four overachieving women who are recovering perfectionists, we've all been slapped in the face with the harsh reality that being

"The Perfect Woman" comes with a hefty price tag. We've also witnessed it with clients who come to us seeking our professional guidance. There's no shortage of extraordinary women who have become so distracted with what they perceive as major shortcomings that they've lost the ability to appreciate their many gifts and celebrate their successes. As time marches on, this begins to manifest as emotional, psychological, and even physical pain.

When the four of us were reflecting on ways that we could help women release their grip on idealism and find ways to live happier, more fulfilling lives, we recognized that *another* self-help book with endless to-do lists would not be the solution. We wanted to take women on a very different journey down a less-traveled path that leads to unconditional self-acceptance. This path is paved with humor, tolerance, and forgiveness, and every step of this journey is transformational in its own right.

Given that the life of a typical overachiever is already filled with self-imposed expectations and too many commitments, the question becomes, how can we simplify this journey? We pondered this question over several bottles of wine and were reminded by our resident landscaping expert, Wendy Lomme, that the most obvious solution would be to mimic nature.

Nature has an enviable way of creating order out of that which seems chaotic and random. We see it with animals, plants, insects, and even microorganisms. It may not look perfect to the casual observer, like grass that goes dormant and turns brown in the summer. This flies in the face of all those brilliant cover shots from our favorite landscaping magazines, where summer parties are being hosted on perfectly manicured lawns that look like green velvet carpet. But grasses are actually designed to go dormant for periods of time when water is scarce. It's a perfectly natural response to the stress of heat and drought.

Nature constantly provides us with cues on how to create a more harmonious existence—we just have to pay attention. This book is organized by season because the seasonal transitions remind us that the only thing that's constant is change. It's perfectly normal (and healthy!) to trust in your instincts and innate wisdom to guide you on your personal journey. Every tip, idea, and anecdote in this book is meant to encourage you to do just that. Each season features a section on mind, body, environment, and connection to nature. Some of the sections will resonate more than others, and you might even find that your attitude toward a particular season differs from what is described in that section. For some, the seasons may have a very literal meaning; for others, it will be more metaphorical. The good news is that you can apply any aspect of any section of this book to your life at the time you need it most (regardless of the season).

Consider starting a journal as an accompaniment to this book. You can use it for the exercises and activities recommended, and you can also make notes and elaborate on concepts that are meaningful to you. The intent is not for you to complete every single action item, but rather to tune in and focus on the ones that inspire and speak to you.

As four recovering perfectionists, we laughed, cried, and simply, yet profoundly, changed our own lives through the writing of this book by heeding one another's guidance. It is our hope that you, too, will design a life that is authentic and rich, leaving you light and full of energy.

Chapter 1

Spring

Shaking the House
and Burning the Devil

"The deep roots never doubt spring will come."
—*Marty Rubin*

Spring is exciting! It's a season of emergence, change, and growth. The ground is literally buzzing with lots of new energy as the plants and animals peak out from hibernation. In spring, we can find a perfect recipe for growth—delightful nourishment from the rains and the comfort of warmer weather. The new energy encourages us to explore and discover the hidden gems of this season—bulbs pushing up from the ground, brightly colored leaf buds on bare branches, and the smell of fresh, warm rain.

It reminds us that no matter how dark and harsh your winter, there's always a light at the end of the tunnel. With rain comes new hope to remind us to dig deep in our hearts to unearth our dreams that have been incubating through winter. It's time to get a move on, take action, and motivate with mind, body, and soul.

In spring you will:

- Fearlessly create authentic vision.
- Cultivate a great relationship with food and your body.
- Create your ever-expanding Peace Zone.
- Reconnect with your garden.

Finding Your Inner Groundhog

Chieko Watanabe, Life Coach

"People are like stained-glass windows. They sparkle and shine
when the sun is out, but when the darkness sets in their true beauty is
revealed only if there is light from within."
—*Elizabeth Kübler-Ross*

Just like the groundhog that goes into hibernation during the winter, our visions go through a period of dormancy. As the metaphorical spring approaches, we mentally and emotionally prepare to emerge into the world with our new vision. We have dreams of amazing relationships we want to cultivate, exciting career directions we wish to take, or the ultimate person we would like to be. The key is to know that you don't need a fully formed, crystal-clear vision before you come out of the burrow. Being out in the world with your new vision is how you gain clarity on the details of what you'd like to have and create for yourself.

You do, however, need to have one thing in place to come out of the burrow and into the world. Unlike the groundhog, you can't be afraid of your shadow and retreat back into your burrow for another six weeks. Moving toward a vision means making a decision. It means acknowledging and owning what you'd really like in your life with no apologies. Sometimes as women we feel silly or guilty for what we want, so we deny ourselves the things we secretly want and don't tell people because of what they might think of us. What the groundhog doesn't know is that your shadow is supposed to be there. It's supposed to be a little scary to emerge into the world with what you truly desire.

Redefine Selfish

Would you like to be let in on a big secret to happiness? Wanting more doesn't mean you're selfish. Wanting more doesn't mean that you aren't already incredibly grateful for everything that you have. Wanting more is about becoming more. Only by becoming more can you truly be of service, live with purpose, and make the positive impact you were put on this earth to have. When you embrace your wants, your crazy ideas, and your supersized vision, you also inspire and give permission for other women to do the same.

You see, most of us have this selfish thing backwards. We think that pursuing what we want is selfish, egotistical, and self-indulgent. I'm not talking about superficial wants like a live-in massage therapist available at your every whim (though there's no reason you can't have this, too). I'm talking about the inspired desires—the desire to be creative, the desire to help people, the desire to be successful, the desire for more love, the desire for more joy and happiness.

This idea that pursuing desires is selfish couldn't be further from the truth. The truth is that NOT going after what you want and NOT living your purpose is selfish. You are putting your fears, insecurities, and doubts over other people's need for your gifts, for the purpose of why you were put here on this earth. You are basically saying, "Nope! Sorry, my fears are more important than being in service to the world!"

Here's something you and the groundhog should know. You're going to see your shadow sometimes, and it's supposed to be scary. Any time you show up fully with your heart's desires, there's the possibility of failure, rejection, and ridicule. The closer this vision is to your heart, the scarier it will feel. Rather than seeing it as a stop or yield sign, know that it's really a green light. When you feel that fear, it's a good sign that you are on the right track and that you are really zeroing in on your heart's desires.

In my own life, I once went on a blind date set up by my friend. I was excited. I picked out a dress, did my hair, and had a nice time. Shortly after, I went on another date with a man I had known for a few years and always thought was incredibly attractive. This time, I was a nervous wreck. I tried on everything in my closet, and nothing seemed good enough. I spent hours giving myself a mani-pedi and doing my hair and makeup to get it just right. It was so much more nerve-racking because I had more on the line. It was scarier because it mattered more to me. I felt *exposed*.

Similarly, what matters most to us is often scariest to pursue. We waste a lot of time chasing things that sort of matter or don't matter at all—and then we wonder why we are living a life of mediocrity that seems to be filled to the brim with chaos.

Let Go of Mediocrity

What would happen if you filled your life with only the things that mattered the absolute most and let go of the sort-of-important and not-at-all-important stuff? How amazing would your life be?

This is about raising your personal standards to no longer accept what you don't want while making the things you do want an absolute MUST. So rather than accepting a mediocre relationship that's not fulfilling, or accepting the fact that you're unhappy at your job, change your standards to say, "I MUST have a loving and fulfilling relationship. I MUST have a job that is aligned with who I am. This is no longer a wish, but something that I will not live without."

As human beings, we really struggle when we are not living out of integrity. We will do anything to stay consistent with whom we believe ourselves to be. If you believe that you are destined to be in volatile, stressful relationships, that is exactly what you will find. If you believe that you can't make the income that you really want, you'll find ways to make that true. To create real, lasting change, change your standards first.

Create New Standards

If you're not sure that you can live up to your new standards, it's a sign that you absolutely should. Living up to your desired standards can be daunting at first, but it's the best way to build self-esteem and gain respect—from yourself and others. Here are some examples of how you might raise your standards:

Old Standard:
I let myself procrastinate often.
New Standard:
I plan well and get things done with time to spare.
Result:
Peace of mind, confidence, satisfaction.

Old Standard:
I take care of everyone, so I don't have time to take care of myself.
New Standard:
Taking care of myself is a MUST, so I have more to give.
Result:
Self-worth, health, more energy.

Curiosity Killed the Critic

Whenever we start anything new—a new job, a new recipe, or a new project—things feel a bit shaky and uncertain at first as we navigate the way. New intentions and new visions will feel like this, too. It's important not to let your inner critic kill your enthusiasm during this delicate time, so that you'll have a fighting chance to step into this vision you are creating. Your inner critic will say things like, "Who do you think you are to want this? You don't know how to do that. You're not good enough to have that. See, you screwed it up again. Just give up and go back to your old life."

What happens to so many of us is that when the going gets rough, we bail, because we can. If the groundhog were truly scared of his shadow and decided never to emerge, it would eventually die, and the truth is, we die, too. When we don't pursue our heart's desires, we slowly die on the inside. When we don't stoke that fire inside ourselves, it starts to die. You've seen people like this. They are functioning members of society with little joy in their hearts and hard faces with hard lines that say, "I'm not happy."

The good news is that there is a powerful and fun way to shut up your inner critic: by being curious and playful and by having fun with the learning process. There will be adventures, new discoveries (both good and bad), times of uncertainty, times when you trip up, and times when you laugh so hard you cry (those are the best, aren't they?). Having a curious and playful nature cannot coexist with your inner critic. Go ahead, try it. Try to feel really curious and critical at the same time. Can't do it, right?

You are seeing the world for the first time with a new filter, a new set of standards, and a new direction. When you change your view of the world, your whole world changes.

Find Your Compass

Start living more simply with ease and peace of mind by letting your heart be your compass, and don't let your mind tell your heart that it's wrong. Your mind is a tool to support and do the work of your heart's desires, not the other way around. And as you step into your vision, continue to use your heart's compass to guide you and your mind to find the best ways to get to your destination.

Action Plan

A vision board is a visual representation of the new vision you intend to create. It's a daily inspiration and reminder of what it is your heart desires. It also activates the Law of Attraction—the idea that like attracts like, and by visualizing what you want you attract it into your life.

Select a poster board or bulletin board and, using pictures, key words, and images, piece together your vision.

What you need:

- A large poster board or bulletin board
- Glue, tape, or tacks to attach your images
- Scissors
- A stack of your favorite magazines
- Quotations, affirmations, key words printed out

Ideas to include on your vision board:

- Pictures of who you would like to be
- Images of things you want or places you'd like to go
- Inspiring quotations and words
- Affirmations you want to experience every day

Tips:

- **Leave your brain out of it.** Don't let your brain make you feel badly for your heart's desires. Make it a judgment-free space and embrace your heart's guidance.
- **Create from an inspired space.** This isn't about creating a masterful work of art or going for perfection. It's about giving your heart the space to breathe and play.

Honoring Your Body Wisdom

Michelle Babb, MS, RD, Nutritionist

"Spring is a new beginning.... The sight of the green color of tender young plants nourishes the soul through the eyes, so the appetite for food decreases and the body naturally cleanses itself, not only of food residues, but of excessive desire and the accompanying emotions of dissatisfaction, impatience, and anger as well. The metaphorical membrane over the eyes and mind disappears, and vision becomes clearer."
— *From* Healing with Whole Foods, *by Paul Pitchford*

Habitual Nourishment vs. Deprivation

Spring is that magical time when we're eager to leave the doldrums of winter behind and move on to new and exciting endeavors. The first warm, sunny day reminds us that soon it will be time to shed the layers of fleece, put away our baggy black sweaters, and get back into sleeveless dresses and eventually swimsuits. Panic ensues! This is prime dieting season, my friends. The media will be beckoning you, priming the pumps with ads that promise you can lose 10 pounds in 10 days with a special diet, a little pill, or a crazy cayenne pepper fast. But this year, you'll be tuning that out, opting for sanity and a logical, foolproof plan to nourish yourself wisely. This is a plan that ignores calorie counting and laughs in the face of tasteless, frozen entrees. It's a plan to eat fresh, colorful, clean food, close to its natural state. You won't lose 10 pounds in 10 days, but you will create a manageable plan that is sustainable for a lifetime. You can permanently delete the word *diet* from your lexicon.

One definition of the word *diet* is "a regimen of eating and drinking sparingly so as to reduce one's weight." Yuck! Everything about that sentence implies that short-term, methodical deprivation is the key to weight loss. Nothing could be further from the truth. A better definition of the word *diet* is "habitual nourishment." Learning how to nourish yourself using your innate wisdom is what transforms you from a chronic dieter into a full-time healthy eater who naturally hovers at a desirable weight.

Let Nature Be Your Culinary Instructor

Use nature as your guide. Think about the lessons that spring can teach you about your eating habits. As Paul Pitchford states in his famous book *Healing with Whole Foods*, our bodies have a natural tendency to want to eat lighter, cleansing foods in the spring. If you're eating lots of processed foods that are loaded with sugar and additives, I can guarantee your body is sending you unreliable signals. For example, if you start your morning with a sugar-laden coffee drink, you're short-circuiting your natural waking hunger cues and using caffeine as a stimulant to mask the fatigue. This sets the stage for the rest of the day and starts a pattern of less than optimal nourishment. If you were to eat a nice, simple, balanced breakfast, such as an egg scramble with veggies, and then enjoy a small cup of coffee after breakfast, it would have a positive influence on your energy levels and eating patterns throughout the rest of the day.

So let your theme for the season be SIMPLE, CLEAN EATING! Although the harvest is not yet bountiful in the spring, you'll see some of the detoxifying greens like dandelion greens and watercress come into

season. You can enjoy fresh asparagus, basil, and spring peas. It's a good
time to start eating some raw veggies
and colorful salads and go lighter
on meat, grains, and sugary foods. I
encourage my clients to make selec-
tions from the local farmers' market
or sign up for weekly or biweekly
deliveries from a CSA (communi-
ty-supported agriculture).

Cultivate a Healthier Relationship with Food

Every one of us is born with the
inner wisdom to know when we're
hungry and when we're full. It's one
of the most basic survival instincts
we have. Eat to live. But chances are, you've had a number of ex-
ternal influences that have taught
you to eat for a lot of reasons that
have nothing to do with hunger. In
fact, most people who struggle with
weight and compulsive eating report not ever feeling true hunger
and/or having a sense of what it means to feel satisfied after a meal.
Perhaps the good news is that emotional eating is a learned behavior.

Spring into Seasonal Eating

Enjoy these nourishing foods as they make their appearance in the spring:

- Asparagus
- Baby spinach
- Beets
- Cauliflower
- Cilantro
- Dandelion greens
- English peas
- Garlic greens
- Kale raab
- Leeks
- Mushrooms
- Onions
- Parsnips
- Potatoes
- Radishes
- Rhubarb
- Shallots
- Watercress

Try these delicious recipes and find other favorites on www.eatplaybe.com:

- Roasted Potato Leek Soup
- Spring Pea and Jicama Salad
- Spring Lamb Stew
- Sun-dried Tomato and Asparagus Frittata

You weren't born with an emotional eating gene, but you might come from a long line of relatives who had some crazy ideas about food and eating. Or you may have had a particularly difficult period in your life when you turned to food because it was the best coping mechanism you had at the time. I had a client who would go on a junk-food binge whenever her partner said something disparaging about her weight, which was fairly often. She admitted that it was definitely a form of self-sabotage, but it also felt like a way to rebel against her partner's controlling nature and verbal abuse. It quickly became evident that she needed to deal with her dysfunctional relationship with her partner in order to stop punishing herself with food.

Another client was convinced that chocolate was simultaneously her best friend and her nemesis. She described chocolate as if it were a highly addictive drug. "I have absolutely no self-control when it comes to chocolate," she said. "I can't be left alone with a bag of Hershey's kisses because I won't stop eating until they're gone." This client felt so ashamed of her self-proclaimed chocolate addiction that she was in the habit of hiding chocolate candy in the kitchen. When she was watching TV with her husband, she would sneak into the kitchen during commercials, get a small fix, and return to the couch as though nothing had happened.

I led my client through a mindful eating activity using a small piece of good-quality dark chocolate. I asked her to examine it with her eyes only, noticing the color and texture. Then I asked her to pick it up and notice the weight of the chocolate and how it felt in her hand. Next, I instructed her to take the chocolate up near her nose and inhale deeply, capturing the rich aroma. Finally, I had her place the chocolate in her mouth, close her eyes, and allow the chocolate to melt on her tongue, noticing all the flavors as they presented themselves. When I asked her how she felt after this exercise, a look of shock came over her face and she said, "I feel satisfied!" I asked her to use this mindful eating technique and to bring her chocolate "out of the closet," so to speak. From that time on, she portioned out a small amount of chocolate, sat next to her husband on the couch, and savored every bite. She took the power and control away from the food.

As you start to examine your food culture and let go of some of the beliefs about food that are no longer useful, you'll allow your true physical hunger and satiety cues to emerge. I'm not a fan of constantly recording every morsel of food you put in your mouth, but I do think there's value in doing some journaling to help connect the dots between what you eat, why you eat it, and how it makes you feel. You may even rank where you are on a scale from 1 to 10 when you start eating and stop eating, with 1 being ravenous and 10 being Thanksgiving full. You won't have to do this forever, but journaling for a week can give you some powerful insights into what triggers some of your eating behaviors.

It may also be useful to use the following table for ideas on how to cope with some of the common emotional triggers. This list is the result of a very productive brainstorming session with a group of women I coached through a 12-week anti-diet program to transform relationships with food. Remember: Food is meant to nourish your *body*. Friends, family, spirituality, and meaningful activities are what nourish your *soul*.

Physical Hunger vs. Emotional Hunger

Physical Hunger	
Symptom	**Remedy**
Hunger (experienced below the neck): stomach is growling; blood sugar is low; feeling of emptiness in the stomach	Food

Emotional Hunger	
Symptom	**Remedy**
Anxiety	Exercise; deep breathing; meditation; affirmations
Fear	Talk with trusted friend/family member; pray; meditate; identify irrational thought patterns; set goals
Stress	Meditate; pray; deep breathing; spa time; talk with friends/family members; simplify and learn to say "no"; eliminate the stressor; exercise
Self-loathing	Practice forgiveness and acceptance; speak or write affirmations; replace negative thoughts with positive/empowering thoughts; journal; use nurturing language
Boredom	Recognize and allow or embrace boredom; read a book; volunteer; be active; rest; nap; meditate
Loneliness	Connect with friends; volunteer in the community; spend time with a pet; touch therapy (e.g., massage)

Emotional Hunger	
Symptom	**Remedy**
Depression	Exercise; counseling; look for mind/body imbalance; journal; read *Unstuck* by Dr. James Gordon; enjoy nature; acupuncture
Grief	Grief counseling; reach out for support from friends/family; accept emotional expression; cry; scream
Control (lack of or need for)	Give it up to the universe; examine the need for control; identify elements of life that feel "out of control"; refer to Serenity Prayer*
Restlessness	Exercise/release it; identify the source
Reward/praise	Identify non-food forms of reward; spa day; travel; weekend getaway; pedicure; movie; bath; time for self
Access/abundance	Eat mindfully and with intention; keep trigger foods out of the home

God grant me the serenity to accept the things I cannot change; courage to change the things I can; and wisdom to know the difference.

Tend to Yourself with Patience and Kindness

There's just no way around it—change takes time and missteps are to be expected. Transforming your food philosophy and creating a healthier relationship with food is no small task. If you were to plant a vegetable garden in your backyard and you brought in the soil, planted the seeds, watered, and fertilized, would you expect to wake up the next morning to a bounty of fresh vegetables ready to harvest? No, because you know that the seeds need time, energy, and nourishment to germinate and grow, and you know that there will be weeds and pests to manage. The same is true of your nutrition and wellness plan. Try to think of the time and energy you put into this as an investment in self-care and extend yourself some patience and kindness. Learn to rejoice as each new seedling emerges as a healthy, hearty plant. Celebrate abundance as your garden continues to grow and flourish.

Action Plan

Focus on simple, clean eating and begin to examine your relationship with food.

- **Clear out your pantry** of foods that are highly processed and contain ingredients that you don't recognize or can't pronounce.
- **Add a few new, seasonal veggies** to your food repertoire.
- **Keep a food-mood journal** for one week. You can find a diet and lifestyle journal template at www.eatplaybe.com/resources.
- **Identify two or three flawed beliefs about eating** that are no longer serving you, such as "I have to feel deprived and hungry to lose weight." Once you've identified these flawed beliefs, replace them with a new truth, such as "I lose weight when I choose to nourish myself with satisfying, whole foods."

Claiming, Creating, and Expanding Your Peace Zone

Karen Pfeiffer Bush, Professional Organizer

"Home is where my habits have a habitat."
— *Fiona Apple*

Spring-cleaning is an age-old tradition worldwide. Modern Americans are not unique in the practice of airing out their homes and scouring and scrubbing the nooks and crannies neglected over winter. Our spring-cleaning is typically a practical effort rather than the ritual and spiritual tradition celebrated in many cultures.

Chinese people mark the New Year—the symbolic end of winter—with a cleaning ritual. Their homes are refreshed with a deep clean prior to the first day of the lunar New Year. Not only is it an exercise in cleaning the physical environment, but it's also a symbolic and spiritual practice to eliminate the old and tired to make room for the new and fresh. It has as much to do with clearing as it does with cleaning.

In Iranian culture, there's a tradition called *khaneh takani*, translated as "shaking the house." For two weeks, the entire family works together to clean and clear the home in preparation for the emergence of spring, a time of regeneration.

Guatemalans partake in a tradition, which has much in common with our spring-cleaning, with an interesting twist. It's called *quama* del *diablo*, "burning the devil." They believe the devil resides in the dust and dirt, in corners and in closets. He is energized by garbage, junk, and unused household items. To get him out, you must clear your home of unsanitary and unused items. Garbage is swept outside into a huge pile, sometimes shared by an entire town. A papier-mâché Satan is placed on top of the heap. In grand form, the pile is set ablaze, burning the devil in effigy. While the environmental ramifications of this practice are suspect, the clearing of the dirt and debris from the home is believed to purify the space, soul, and spirit.

Spring-cleaning "American style" is what we do because our mothers and grandmothers always did it. Easter-colored headlines in the checkout line make us feel guilty if we're not dedicating our weekends to the "deep clean" that *must* come with the onset of spring.

Shaking the house, burning the devil, clearing or cleaning the home—whether motivated by the spirit or by a sense of obligation— can produce the same result: rejuvenation, refreshment, a sense of peace. Of course we all want to feel peaceful in a clean and devil-free home. Can we convince our spouses and children to spend two weeks shaking the house? Are our neighbors up for a communal bonfire to collectively burn our trash and unwanted household items? Probably not.

So how do we do it? How do we, without a dedicated holiday or fear of the devil, easily embrace the practice that we know will undoubtedly result in a pleasant outcome—a sense of peace in our home?

Create Your Peace Zone

It's human nature and actually a good idea to stop what you're doing when you aren't experiencing positive results. When faced with overwhelming projects like deep cleaning or re-organizing your entire home, people tend to jump from place to place. They work a little in the basement, a little in the bedroom closet, and a little in the garage, and at the end of a weekend they are exhausted and wonder what exactly they accomplished. Since there's no sign of success, they typically stop dead in their tracks.

I'd like to introduce you to a concept called the Peace Zone. Reader, meet the Peace Zone. Peace Zone, *please* meet the reader.

Definition of the Peace Zone: a place in which you are surrounded *only* by the things that you love, use, or need. The things that you love are there to feed your soul, and the things that you use and need are where you need them for when you need them.

Everyone's Peace Zone Is Unique

Simply put, the Peace Zone is the place where you go to recharge your batteries and become energized. This is different for everyone. No one can tell you where it is or what it should be. Here are some examples.

- **Garage:** a place to tinker and work on projects.
- **Dining room table:** a sacred place for you and your family to share meals and time together. A great place to nurture your relationship with food.
- **Entertainment area:** a place to be energized by the company of others.
- **Bedroom:** the last place you see at night and the first place you see when you wake up in the morning.
- **A chair:** in the corner of the living room where the sun shines "just right."

Your Personal Brand of Peace

In a perfect world, everyone should feel at peace in their entire home. However, most of us do not live in a perfect world. Perfectionism can be a roadblock preventing us from moving forward in business and in life. People often are hung up on the magazine version of home. The photos of rooms arranged by designers can be a great inspiration but can also bring on a sense of inadequacy. "If my house can't look like that, then I'm not going to bother doing anything at all."

Your brand of perfect and peace is just that—your brand. If you smile and feel warm inside by seeing the pictures of your niece and nephew on your fridge or your collection of baseball hats on a coat rack in your hall, then that is peace.

I recently worked with a client (we'll call her Jan) who cleared her mantle of dusty and tired candles and tchotchkes that had accumulated over the years. She decided that not one of them meant a thing to her. Jan replaced them with her treasured collection of porcelain pigs that was in a box in her closet for ten years. They are lined up in size order on her fireplace mantle and she is thrilled. You might say, "When pigs fly will there be porcelain pigs on my mantle," but for her, this is peace. By the way, she actually has a couple of flying pigs, too. Jan smiles every time she looks at them.

In my house, my kids do art on the dining room table. I once set up an adorable art studio in my basement. My kids would lug the supplies upstairs and work at the dining table to be near all the action. Guess where those supplies would stay when something else drew their attention? Finally, I decided to stop fighting it. I got a pretty piece of furniture that coordinates with my dining room and filled it with their art supplies. They now have access to their supplies and can walk a foot away to return them when they're done. In a perfect world, they'd do this without reminders. Ha! So what if the furniture store called it a jewelry armoire? It is perfect for art supplies, looks good in my dining room, and most important, works for us. That gives me peace in my home.

What gives you peace? What artwork, pillows, photos, or collections warm your heart? Why aren't they out, center stage, where you can see them? If they are out, what other meaningless things are stealing the show?

In addition to surrounding yourself with the things you love, need, and use, it's crucial to eliminate the things that you do not love, need, or use.

The Ever-Expanding Peace Zone

Jan, my sweet, pig-collecting client, had an epiphany when she realized how happy her mantle made her feel. It was the Peace Zone that she identified early on in her organizing project. She then moved on to the bookshelf alongside her fireplace and eliminated the dusty old books that she forgot were even there. She replaced them with a gallery of family photos. This made her even happier. All the while, she resisted the urge to drop her mail on the mantle because her pig display became sacred. Every week she dusted her photo frames. She had pillows made out of her grandmother's embroidery and placed them on her sofa. No longer did she toss her jackets and purse on the sofa. A collection of old *Saturday Evening Post* magazines that once sat in a box sits on her coffee table in place of the piles of unread catalogs.

Over time, she moved bit by bit through her living room, and then the rest of her home. Jan eliminated the unwanted and unneeded to make an adorable space that warms her heart and, frankly, mine. I think it should be featured in a magazine. Her home is truly her Peace Zone. She can relax and recharge her batteries there. For the first time in five years, she's proud of her home and has friends over.

The point in identifying a single Peace Zone is to have a place to start. Eventually, you will move outward from your original Peace Zone, allowing it to spread throughout your home. So pick that shelf or corner, workbench or table, and proudly declare it as your Peace Zone. Get rid of the stuff that doesn't matter to you and display only the things that you love. Treat it as sacred because what you love "lives" there. You'll see—your Peace Zone will spread!

The Victories of Small Battles

Because we don't have a holiday dedicated to "shaking the house," we need to schedule our home projects. But who the heck has time? Now hear this: you don't have to take a sabbatical from work, send your kids away to the grandparents, or even dedicate a weekend to "attack your house." The best-fought wars have been won by the victories of small battles. You may not believe this yet, but if you spend just 15 minutes a day focused on creating peace in your home, you will achieve it faster than if you launch a full-blown attack during a weekend.

15 Minutes to Peace

1. Write your daily 15-minute work sessions in your calendar.
2. Boldly say out loud your new mantra: "I can do anything for 15 minutes!"
3. Pick your Peace Zone. Start small with a shelf, drawer, or small pile.
4. Set your timer for 15 minutes.
5. Remove everything that you do not love, need, or use from that space, and sort them into categories:
   - Give away
   - Throw away
   - Put away (somewhere else)
6. The give-away items should go into a small box or bag. When the box or bag is full, march it right out to your car and place on the passenger seat to be dropped off at the donation site the next time you go out.
7. The throw-away items should be thrown away immediately.
8. The put-away items should be put away where they will be loved, needed, or used. You may not have a perfect location yet for some things, but just get them out of your Peace Zone and close to the area where other like items live or where they will be used. Put your screwdriver near other tools. Put your reading glasses near your reading chair. Put your stamps near your checkbook or stationery.
9. Go back to the little area of your Peace Zone and arrange the items that remain there into a pleasing display. This is not a design competition. Arrange the little shelf, table, or corner of the desk in a way that you like.

Ding! Your 15 minutes are up and you have taken the first step to creating or recapturing your Peace Zone.

If you feel energized and have the time, I'm not going to stop you from setting that timer for another 15 minutes. If you don't have time, it's okay. Tomorrow is another day with another 15 minutes. For your next "session," move down to the next shelf or over to the next 6 inches of desk space. The key is to move geographically through the area—inch by inch, bite by bite— achieving small but noticeable successes along the way. As you clear and create each small section of your Peace Zone, leaving only the things you love, need, and use there, treat the cleared spaces as sacred. Keep and appreciate the way that you arranged each space as you move on to the next area.

The more times that your 15-minute timer dings, the larger your Peace Zone will become. It will radiate outward from the epicenter. Pretty soon, your entire bedroom or kitchen or TV room will be a Peace Zone filled only with the things that you love, need, and use. Eventually, bit by bit, your entire home can be free of the old and tired and you will have a clean, clear, devil-free, shaken house—your very own Peace Zone.

The 15 minutes a day decluttering concept adapted from FlyLady.net.

Action Plan

Identify your Peace Zone and work in 15-minute sessions to free it of anything you do not love, need, or use. Arrange the remaining loved or useful items in a pleasing way.

Note from a Client

Hi Karen,

One of my very favorite things about travel comes to mind as I pack to come home from my trip. I've always loved this about travel: everything in its place, no chaos, everything neat . . . that's how I've been living for the past nine days in LA. On nearly every trip, I contemplate what it would be like and would it be possible to live like this at home. I know now, thanks to you, that the path to this is an ever-expanding Peace Zone. AND changing the behaviors that lead to the accumulation of things.

Janet

Rediscovering the Outdoors
(a.k.a. What Do You Mean I Have a Yard?)
Wendy Lomme, Landscape Designer

And Spring arose on the garden fair,
Like the Spirit of Love felt everywhere;
And each flower and herb on Earth's dark breast
rose from the dreams of its wintry rest.
— *Percy Bysshe Shelley, "The Sensitive Plant"*

There's a reason landscaping companies see a significant increase in phone calls and communication from prospective clients in the spring. It's what I like to call the *I-Forgot-I-Had-a-Yard* syndrome. After huddling indoors for the winter, trudging from home to car to work to car to home, one dry day is all it takes to coax us from our caves. Everything about spring is different: the air smells fresh and clean, the colors of nature's palette look richer, and the world is brighter with longer and drier days. Now that you've remembered what your neighbors look like, it's time to embrace all that spring has to offer.

Hunting for Bulbs

In early spring, the signs of winter are still evident, especially in soggy leaves still covering the ground. That ugly brown mess might be hiding a special treat—one of the first signs of life from the soil. It seems to happen overnight. The bright green, tender shoots start pushing their way through the surface. Once you take notice, they are everywhere!

If you missed out on planting bulbs outdoors in the fall, it's not too late. One of my favorite ways to bring the inspiration of spring into my world is to grow bulbs indoors. You can plant one or a few bulbs in the "traditional" method, in a pot with soil. Or you can try the water method:

- Pick your bulb: hyacinth, narcissus, and crocus are reliable water bloomers.
- For hyacinth and crocus, use any glass or vase that will hold the bulb suspended at the top of the vessel.
- For narcissus, use a bowl and "plant" the bulbs in pebbles.
- Keep the water level about one-quarter of the way up from the bottom of the bulb.

This Bush Is on Fire!

While bulbs are a well-known way to enjoy spring, a more subtle form of inspiration is noticing budding leaves. On deciduous plants and trees, the branches are bare through the winter, but they start showing signs of life with warmer temperatures. My favorite plant to watch is *Spiraea japonica*, which is one of the earliest to bud. A few of the varieties actually look like they are on fire, with their upright branches and bright red leaf buds. I call this my indicator plant, providing inspiration and hope that summer is just around the corner.

Spiraea japonica may be *my* indicator plant, but there are many others more easily found. I can always count on the same question each spring from my mom, who lives in New England. "Is your forsythia blooming yet?" That is her indicator plant, even if the bright yellow blossoms are suspended above a few feet of snow.

The Japanese tradition of *hanami* has spread around the globe, bringing beauty and excitement to springtime. *Hanami* literally means "picnicking under a blossoming cherry tree," but in many countries it means festivals and celebrations to observe, admire, and cherish the beautiful blooms.

Observing and admiring plants is second nature to most of us, but

A River Runs Through It

You can emulate a natural spring in your yard by creating a dry river creek. Use natural stone, like round river rocks and small boulders, to create the illusion of a meandering stream. To create a successful dry river creek:

- Observe your yard during heavy rains: where is the water naturally flowing?
- Follow the natural contours of your yard, keeping in mind that water always chooses the easiest route.
- Dig a shallow trench for the river rock to sit in to create a natural look.
- Use various stone sizes that are proportionate to your yard.

some might ask (ahem, Chieko), "Who cares?!" Why do we feel such a connection to plants? Why bother standing around and looking at them? Part of the admiration, especially for mature trees and plants (which may be several hundred or several thousand years old), is their ability to survive without much help. In fact, they usually survive *in spite of* harsh conditions and environmental degradation. For younger plants and trees we grow ourselves, we can easily relate to them as living creatures. They need food, water, and some degree of shelter to survive. They can communicate their needs, if we are keen enough to notice: wilting if they need water, yellowing if they are overwatered, losing a limb if they are injured or diseased. And, if we succeed in nurturing and growing a plant, we feel a sense of pride, accomplishment, and contribution to the world.

The Amazing Seed

Spring is a magical time of year. There is activity happening everywhere outdoors, both seen and unseen. I am in awe of the plants, especially the tender ones, which survive the brutal winter to emerge strong and ready to grow, bloom, and thrive. If you've ever grown a plant from a seed, you know how vulnerable the young plants are. Seeds are absolutely amazing. Did you happen to hear about the *32,000*-year-old seed that was discovered and germinated in 2012?! Prior to that, the oldest germinated seed was about 2,000 years old.

Even you non-plant geeks can surely respect the power of the amazing seed, such little things holding so much life for thousands of years. Making a comeback with gardeners are the heirloom seeds. Successfully grown heirloom fruits and vegetables taste incredible. When you embark on the wonderful experience of growing heirloom plants, saving the seeds and growing new plants the next year, you become part of the magic. As an added benefit, you truly know where your food is coming from.

Last summer, I was gifted an heirloom Italian tomato plant that produced beautiful, delicious tomatoes. I didn't want this to be a one-summer-only event, so I saved some of the seeds to bring me more amazing tomatoes for summers to come. *Mangia!*

Dirty Workout

Gardening and nourishment go hand in hand. Many people experience weeding as meditation, given the repetitive and calming motions that are involved. It is the perfect way to feed your mind, body, and soul, to reconnect with the earth and feel a sense of accomplishment. Many years ago, when I was paid to play in the dirt, I would proudly proclaim that my job was my gym membership. I was paid to do squats (picking up/putting down potting soil, wall blocks, etc.). I burned calories raking and shoveling, and I even found time to stretch while watering hanging baskets.

These days, I embrace a more casual tempo when working in my own yard. I definitely take more breaks, and even practice some yoga moves to make sure I'm in tune with my body. Why not throw in a Down Dog before you start weeding? Or practice some Cat/Cow in between planting your veggies? I love being able to let my mind wander while I'm pruning and weeding. A few yoga moves are the perfect way to make sure my body is being nurtured too. Spring is the time of year to ease into outdoor activities. Let inspiration, and the somewhat unpredictable weather, guide you.

Party While You Work!

Consider organizing a work party with a few of your neighbors; work in their yard for a set amount of time, and then move to the next yard. Not only can you help each other with two- (or more) person tasks, but you will also benefit from another set of eyes to get every last weed or decide where to install a new plant. Also, the conversation can help mundane tasks go quickly!

Action Plan

- Apply Karen's concept of the Peace Zone to your yard. Set your timer for 15 minutes and start tackling one area of your yard. It might be the area that makes you cringe every time you walk by it, or it might be near your favorite tree that is about to bloom. Start small so you can be encouraged by your progress!

- Create a plan; try envisioning your space on paper. Draw a simple sketch of what you have and make note of the things that work and the aspects that aren't working. Draw a second "blank slate" sketch and record your dream yard. Use this plan to achieve your dream bit by bit, plant by plant!

- Plant indoor bulbs to bring the beauty closer to home.

- Consider using heirloom plants and seeds for your edibles.

- Find your indicator plant and keep it with you to provide hope and inspiration. Take a picture, take clippings to display indoors, or plant one to enjoy for years to come.

Chapter 2

Summer

Unpacking Your Fun Box

"Summer afternoon—summer afternoon; to me those have always been the two most beautiful words in the English language."
—*Henry James*

Finally! It seems we wait all year for summer to come. This is where all our hard work from spring pays off and we're rewarded with sunshine and lazy days! The earth is in its juicy fruition and abundance. Plants and trees are at their peak, fully grown for the year and fruiting or blooming for our senses to enjoy. As the heat of summer moves in, it gives us a chance to slow down and truly enjoy the richness and fullness of the abundant earth.

Summer is a time of celebration. Play! Party! Have fun! Shed the layers of winter and jump into the cool, refreshing lake of celebration and splash around!

In summer you will:

- Fall in love with imperfection.
- Savor three new ingredients for meals: love joy, and mindfulness.
- Pack a box of fun.
- Reimagine your outdoor living space.

Discovering Life Really IS a Beach
Chieko Watanabe, Life Coach

"There are only two ways to live your life. One is as though nothing is a miracle. The other is as though everything is a miracle."
—*Albert Einstein*

Summer is a time of happiness. We expect the summer sun to shine in the sky and also in our hearts. The birds will sing to us on the branches just outside the window. We'll have picnics on checkered picnic blankets out by the lake and sticky ice cream cones in the afternoon.

The perfection of a gorgeous summer day is truly alluring. I dream of perfectly tan skin, a bikini-tight figure, and expertly manicured toes tucked into cork wedge sandals while I lay out my beautiful picnic of homemade apple pie and crustless sandwiches.

Living in Seattle has taught me to set more realistic expectations. Summer doesn't begin until July 5th. We get no more than three extra-hot days in August. And never, ever put away your raincoat because as soon as you do, you'll need it.

The truth is, summer is a time to let go of all the drive for perfection, step into the rays of receiving and celebrating, and let the warmth of our imperfect lives wash over us. It's a time to be exposed as who we are, authentically and unapologetically.

Summer isn't a time for striving but for living in the moment, being present with ourselves and the people around us, and allowing for the beauty of what's happening in all its imperfect glory to shine through. It's about being in the sun and getting sunburned despite the SPF 50 you've been slathering on all day, watching the ants jonesing for the berry tart that you worked so hard to prepare the night before, feeling sticky and sweaty with sand in your bikini bottoms, and loving it all the same.

Celebrate Island Style

When I go to visit my sister, who lives on Oahu, there's a dead giveaway of tourists versus locals on the beach. The tourists show up with cooler in hand, big bright towels, bottles of SPF in lotion AND spray form, enough floaty beach blow-up thingies for a small aqua army, a volleyball net, a Frisbee, and a video camera. The locals show up with nothing more than a raggedy old towel.

You see, summer can't be concocted through perfect accessories. Summer isn't about creating perfect experiences. It's about embracing and celebrating what is. The locals know that the beach is the beach and they don't try to make it into their living rooms. They celebrate the beach for exactly what it is: a sandy, dirty, salty mess with bugs, crabs, and cigarette butts right next to the crystal clear aquamarine waters of the Pacific Ocean.

Celebrating in the moment is also about celebrating who you are just as you are. It's a time to let go of your old beliefs about beauty. *"When I lose 10 pounds, then I will be beautiful." "If I get Botox, then I will be beautiful." "When I get bigger boobs, then I'll be beautiful."* I challenge you to see your beauty as you are right now, without changing a thing. Summer is a great time to stop chasing for cover model perfection (it's a race we can't win—without Photoshop, anyway) and choose to feel beautiful in your own skin. You know you are celebrating the moment and your true beauty when you feel beautiful despite your bad haircut, the extra pounds around your middle, and the breakouts, sunburn, and rashes on your skin.

Being in the moment might sound a bit esoteric, but really it's quite simple and a grounding experience. It's the act of being mindful and accepting what is true of the moment. My yoga teacher says that the past is history and the future is fiction. We can let all that go because it doesn't really matter anyway, and be here in the now. Take a moment right now to be aware of your breath, to be with the background noise, the anxious worry you might be carrying in your stomach, and so on. Stop and notice what is going on around you and within you. Are you holding tension in your shoulders or maybe your jaw? Are your feet tired? Allow your authentic experience to be exposed—if not to the world, then at least to yourself. When you take the time to observe and simply be, you experience life in a real, tangible, grounding way.

My Gratitude Practice

My gratitude practice is deeply personal, as yours will be for you. I encourage you to find your own practice that best supports the grateful gal inside. My gratitude practice begins with my first cup of coffee—I'm so thankful for it. And with each sip, I say a little prayer of thanks for all the abundance in my life—the wonderful, thoughtful man who brings me coffee every morning, my fat cat on my lap, work I love, a cute little car to get me around, and each of my family members and friends.

Attracting the Yummy Things

What makes the celebration even sweeter and juicier is the delicious practice of gratitude. The practice of gratitude immediately creates a sense of abundance, peace of mind, appreciation, and love, and the best part is, it's really effortless. It's instantaneously transformational and so easy to do.

We can always carry summer in our hearts through the practice of gratitude by recognizing and appreciating all the abundance that we have—abundance in money, health, love, relationships, ideas, culture, creativity, self-expression, and so on. When we direct our attention to these yummy things through the practice of gratitude, we live rich lives, and through the Law of Attraction, we invite even more yummy things, because like attracts like.

Sometimes, there are days when everything seems to go haywire: the kids are bickering, your husband is cranky, traffic is horrible, and your coworkers are uncooperative. On these days it can be hard to call upon those feelings of gratitude. But, even when we're sick, we can be grateful for the medical care that is available to us and the people who help make us well. Even when we are heartbroken, we can be grateful for the lessons we learned in love. Even when we have little money in our bank account, we can be thankful for the roads we drive on, the roof over our head, and the material possessions that we do have. Even when our family ticks us off, we can be grateful for the love, companionship, and connection they provide. There is so much to be grateful for if you take a moment to look. I'm grateful to have eyes to see, for the love in my life, for my education, my family, my health, my youth, my maturity, and oh yes, my beauty just as I am.

Action Plan

- **Celebration practice:** Find something to celebrate every day. Celebration is not measured by a physical act, per se. It's more a mind-set of taking the time and energy to acknowledge achievements, successes, and other wonderful things in life.
- **Gratitude practice:** Come up with three new things you are grateful for every day for one month. It will retrain your mind to always look for things for which you are grateful.

Eating Like a Skinny Person

Michelle Babb, MS, RD, Nutritionist

"French women typically think about good things to eat.
American women typically worry about bad things to eat."
— *Mireille Guiliano, French Women Don't Get Fat: The Secret
of Eating for Pleasure*

Summer is undoubtedly my favorite season. Longer days mean an abundance of light and warmth from the sun. Gardens are overflowing with leafy greens, carrots, radishes, peas, and tomatoes, and we're all ready to devote more time to socializing and enjoying the great outdoors with friends and family.

A magical thing happens the minute summer officially arrives in Seattle and makes its presence known with a full day of blue skies and temperatures over 70 degrees. There's a perceptible shift in the collective mood of Seattleites. People emerge from their caves in cargo shorts and flip-flops, ready to fire up the barbie and take on the world—exposed and beautiful! Aaaah, the wonders of a little vitamin D.

It doesn't take long to start filling up those weekends like a blackout card at a bingo parlor. Before you know it, you're booked through September with all the activities that need to be crammed into those three precious months of cooperative weather. It's no wonder that nutrition often takes a backseat and overindulgence becomes the constant com-

Mindful	Mindless
Knowing where your food comes from.	Believing your food just magically appears at the store.
Preparing a homemade meal.	Receiving your food through a drive-through window.
Sitting down at the table to eat.	Eating while driving.
Focusing on the act of eating.	Multitasking while eating.
Setting the fork down between bites.	Shoveling the food in like it's a race to the finish.
Eating because you're hungry.	Eating just because.
Noticing when you feel satiated.	Eating until you feel sick.

panion of abundance. But guess what . . . there's a way to appreciate abundance while honoring your wellness goals and practicing mindful, intuitive eating, and it's a lot more fun than it sounds.

The Anti-Diet Attitude

The idea of eating healthy all the time is overwhelming and probably not practical for most of us. My husband and I spend a week every year at my in-laws' lake place in Wisconsin, home of the fried cheese curds and more taverns per capita than any other state in the nation. I know that our week at the lake will include more beer, meat, and sweets (and a lot fewer vegetables) than my husband and I would normally consume, but that's okay. Even when I don't have complete control over my food choices, I still have options to make my own food contributions and decide how I want to eat within the context of a different food environment.

During our week at the lake, we do one or two big grocery shopping trips at the local market, plan a couple of dinner meals, cut up some veggies and fruit for healthy snacking, and make a big salad to go along with whatever people choose to have for lunch. My nieces and nephews get in on the food prep and cooking, and it's gratifying to watch the whole family gobbling up fruit and making a place on their plates for salad.

Whenever I feel like I have less control over *how* I'm eating (e.g., dining out at a tavern in a small Wisconsin town), I just try to make reasonably good choices from the limited options and focus more on conversing and celebrating with family and friends. Even in scenarios where the food offerings are less than ideal, you have a choice to be mindful and present versus checking out and adopting the "if you can't beat 'em, join 'em" attitude.

You'll be relieved to know that mindful eating has nothing to do with being perfect. It has everything to do with being intentional and purely present, moment to moment, while you're selecting, preparing, and eating your food. I once worked with a client—we'll call her Sarah—who had the goal of breaking a lifelong dieting pattern and becoming an intuitive eater. She had lost 30 pounds and was doing extremely well changing her mind-set about food when she was confronted with a trip to New York with a bunch of girlfriends. Sarah was very concerned about being able to practice her newly acquired mindful eating skills while dining out and celebrating with friends.

When she returned, Sarah came into my office beaming with pride. When I asked about her trip she exclaimed, "I ate like a skinny person!" I asked what that meant and she told me that she did not restrict herself by saying she couldn't have this or that, but she sampled small portions and truly enjoyed every morsel of food she put in her mouth and every sip of wine that she took. Not only did she have the satisfaction of realizing that she was actively ditching her dieting mentality once and for all, but she also lost three pounds while on vacation! Sarah made deliberate food choices that did not feel depriving and she did a lot of walking.

This new mind-set that Sarah described is the premise for books like *French Women Don't Get Fat*. It's as much about attitude as it is about what you're choosing to eat. Despite what the $60 billion dieting industry would have you believe, you don't get fit and healthy from living in a state of constant deprivation and semi-starvation. You get there by eating nourishing foods, feeding your body when you're physically hungry, savoring decadent foods that are meant to be treats, and living an active lifestyle. Summer happens to be the perfect season to start practicing this new anti-diet attitude!

Your Own Local Food Movement

One surefire way to be more mindful and intentional about your food choices is to experiment with eating more locally grown foods. If you choose to take Wendy's advice from the spring chapter and plant your own vegetable garden, you can just waltz right into your own yard and gather ingredients for a meal. It doesn't get any more local than that! But if you're short on growing space or time, or you're just agriculturally challenged, you can still create your own movement within your household to eat mostly what local farmers are growing.

My favorite way of getting more in touch with how my food is produced is to visit my local farmers' market on Sunday mornings. It gives me a chance to chat with farmers, get tips on how to prepare some of the more unusual or unfamiliar veggies, and get a sense for what's truly in season. Plus, I can feel good about supporting organic farmers in my own community. This is a big part of what makes those summer Sundays my favorite day of the week! I leave the market with a beautiful basket of freshly harvested, brightly colored foods and plans to create my own delicious masterpiece.

You might also consider doing something like the 100-mile challenge for a few weeks or a month in the summer. This is a relatively new movement where you try to eat only what's produced within 100 miles of your home. You will most assuredly learn a lot more about where your food comes from, and it can be a very educational exercise for the whole family. Thankfully, we have a lot of beautiful farms

Joy in the Kitchen

Use these tips to make meal preparation and cooking more enjoyable:

- Organize your kitchen and make it into a functional space that you enjoy. Note: This does not require major remodeling. A good cleaning, a fresh coat of paint, and some cleared countertops are all you need.
- Share the responsibility of food preparation by getting all family members involved. Small children can help with simple tasks like tearing lettuce for a salad, and older kids can participate in more complex cooking activities.
- Have a theme night once a week or once a month and inspire yourself and your family to cook different types of ethnic foods.
- Have your spouse or partner help wash and chop veggies when you get home from the grocery store so you have lots of fresh ingredients that are ready to use with little or no prep. Turn on the music, dance around the kitchen, and have fun with it!
- Reimagine some of your old family recipes, such as Shepherd's Pie and Green Bean Casserole, to make healthier versions that can become new food traditions.
- Take a cooking class!

and wineries within a 100-mile radius of Seattle, so there's not much we have to live without.

Ready to be inspired? Check out the blogs related to the 100-mile diet and/or read the book *The 100-Mile Diet: A Year of Local Eating* by Alisa Smith and J.B. MacKinnon. Another very relevant and fun read is *Animal, Vegetable, Miracle* by Barbara Kingsolver.

A Love Infusion

Another critical aspect of good self-nourishment has to do with food preparation. I've worked with hundreds of clients and have seen cooking skills that range from those barely able to turn on the stove to people who can chef it up with nothing more than a potato and a can of stewed tomatoes. You certainly don't have to be an Iron Chef to take pleasure in the act of cooking or food preparation, but it helps if you are willing to see the value in assembling your own fresh ingredients and have some fun along the way.

The most powerful example of mindful food preparation I can think of is Masaru Emoto's book *The Hidden Messages in Water*. Emoto conducted an experiment in which he labeled containers of water with certain words, some positive (like love, joy, and friendship) and others negative (like hate, fear, and war). He then froze the containers of water and later examined them under a microscope, and the results were astonishing. Without exception, the ice crystals that formed in the containers with positive words were magnificent, beautiful structures that looked like works of art. The water in the containers labeled with negative words, however, formed chaotic, grotesque crystal structures. Some actually resembled cancerous tumors.

The water in Emoto's famous experiment came from one source and all other variables were controlled, so the only explanation is that the words and the energy associated with those words and thoughts had a powerful influence on the final product. Isn't it possible, or perhaps even probable, that when we're making a meal feeling joyful and grateful we're actually infusing love into the food and transforming the molecules in our food in a positive way?

Conversely, if we're full of negativity and resentment while preparing a meal it could be showing up in our food in unexpected ways. Even if you're not quite buying the results of Emoto's study and you don't believe in the energetic properties of food, you can probably agree that it is more enjoyable for everyone involved if meal preparation is a more positive experience.

Action Plan

Use the following mindful eating activity to help you get in the habit of being more present during the act of self-nourishment:

Mindful Eating Activity
1. Create a beautiful, healthy meal made from foods you love to eat.
2. Set the table with linens, candles, or whatever you have that makes it feel like a special meal.
3. Arrange the food on your plate as you would see in a restaurant.
4. Put some music on (or enjoy the silence) and sit down to your meal.

5. Notice the way the food looks on your plate.

6. Pay attention to the aromas and notice whether you can pick out any individual ingredients.

7. Take the first bite and really tune in to the texture and flavors. Try to chew slowly and notice how the food changes as you chew.

8. Swallow and notice the sensation as the food moves through your digestive tract.

9. Continue to eat the rest of your meal in this mindful way, engaging all of your senses.

After the meal, answer these questions:

1. What was the best part about your mindful eating experience?

2. What was the most challenging part?

3. How does this differ from how you normally eat?

Planned Spontaneity

Karen Pfeiffer Bush, Professional Organizer

"Look at me!
Look at me!
Look at me NOW!
It is fun to have fun
But you have to know how!"
—*Dr. Seuss,* The Cat in the Hat

Summer is here! Aaah! Finally . . . the easy, breezy days of sipping lemonade on the porch, last-minute barbecues, and spontaneous day or weekend trips to the beach. Reality? Not for all.

Personally, I love the idea of last-minute guests and impromptu events and activities. I'll be honest, though: this does not come naturally to me. I'm a Planner! This is a title that suits me well in most of life's pursuits. It has, however, been known to stand in the way of the dream I have of dropping everything and saying, "Let's go wherever the wind takes us!"

The first time I tried to embrace this idea, my kids were thrilled and my husband stared at me like I'd lost my mind, wondering if I'd undergone a personality transplant while he was at work. My family was aghast because the wind doesn't take our minivan anywhere. The Planner behind the wheel knows exactly where she's going and exactly what we will need when we get there—on time.

On the sly, I quickly confessed to my husband that I was faking the wind-taking-us-anywhere idea. There are worse things to lie to your children about, right? I'll be honest (*with you*). I've learned to embrace spontaneity, *with a little advance planning.* I know, I know. This is the greatest oxymoron in the history of the world, but I truly believe that I'm tricking my planning gene by faking it 'til I make it. It's *really* fun!

If you're a Planner or Not-So-Much-a-Planner (NSMP), a little organizing can go a long way toward being ready to jump feet first into summer. Don't fear, NSMPs, this is fun organizing versus what you may sometimes find to be agonizing organizing.

Goodbye Perfectionism, Hello Funorganizing!

Before we get into this concept of "funorganizing," it's important to the Planners and the NSMPs to once again address the issue of perfectionism. You know, that little something that sometimes stands in the way of forward progress. It's thoughts like "My house won't look like a design magazine spread, so I'm not going to do anything at all to it" or "I don't have time to make my apartment look perfect, so I'm not going to have friends over for happy hour tonight." How many of your friends actually believe that your place always looks perfect? How many of them have a perfect home? And, by the way, who's to say what's perfect?

Let's say you have friends over when your home is not magazine perfect. In ten years, will they remember the papers on the desk or the toys on the floor? Or will they remember that epic happy-hour-turned-dance-party way back when? Or the neighborhood-potluck-turned-kickball-tournament? And to think that those memories would never have been created if you had been hung up on the design magazine image or had to prep for days to entertain at your home. The thought of a party gone un-had is so sad. But it happens, people!

As a Planner, I envy you laid-back NSMPs. Many of you have it dialed in just right. Fun opportunities don't often elude you because you are not hung up on how they're supposed to go. Until I got to know more of you in my professional organizing career, I believed that all NSMPs were able to jump feet first into the unplanned unknown. I now know that not all of you are using your natural gift to enjoy and embrace the unstructured and impromptu without getting stuck on those pesky details. Some of you feel that you should be a Planner and therefore don't do anything at all.

NSMPs may envy the Planners for always having it all worked out and being prepared. Many Planners do throw awesome parties with every wonderful detail addressed. If you're planning a wedding, business party, or specific celebration like a baby shower or graduation, a Planner is your go-to gal.

Sometimes, however, that planning gene gets in the way of spur-of-the-moment fun: the last-minute barbecue, the refrigerator clean-out dinner party, or the get-to-the-beach-before-it-starts-to-rain picnic. If a Planner doesn't feel ready, she may opt out. Sniff!

The Happy Medium

It really isn't as cut-and-dried as being a Planner or being an NSMP. There are those who, by nature or by sheer will to defy their genes, fall into the happy medium category. Of course, there are people representing every level of the scale between pure Planner and pure NSMP, or even switch between the two during different aspects and times of their lives. The truly enviable are those who can find a balance.

The way to trick your inner Planner into being spontaneous or allow your NSMP to take action and have some fun is to do a little advance prep work. Here are some funorganizing tips that will allow the Planners, the NSMPs, and everyone in between to have some summer fun without getting hung up on the details!

Fun Files
- Do some research into fun day or weekend trips and things to do around town.
- Purchase tickets or gift cards in advance for use at museums or activity centers.
- Stock up on online deals, such as Groupon and Living Social, and fundraising auction items. It's a great way to have fun without breaking the bank.
- Create a "Local Fun" file, a "Day Trip Fun" file, and a "Weekend Fun" file.

When the spirit moves you, you can reach into one of those files and have a (preplanned) spontaneous getaway. Having those files is perfect for when you hear or read about a special place or a fun local activity. You can tear out the article, jot down the information, and file it in your fun files. For those of you who are not keen on keeping files of paper, use a scanner and file it in your computer. You can also use online and mobile applications such as Evernote or Pinterest to keep track of your fun ideas.

For a little more planned spontaneity, you can separate by region. I may announce to my family, "We are going where the wind takes us this weekend! Should we head north, south, across the water, or over the mountains?" Once the direction is decided, I'll pull out several activities, ferry schedules, and restaurant or hotel guides that I've collected for that area. I, of course, can't resist a quick phone call to determine hotel availability, but more power to those who can.

What's in Your Fun Box?

Spending a little time to plan for spontaneous opportunities is rewarding. Imagine how prepared you'll feel with a prepacked box of fun that is ready to grab and go. For example, since I started carrying my beach gear in my trunk, it isn't a big deal to just stop at the beach for a little while instead of going home to gather gear (usually too much of it) and then deciding that maybe I just don't have enough time to go after all.

Some of the things in our summer party bucket include a collection of funny cocktail napkins, sparklers, candles, playing cards and dice,

Fun Boxes

The On-the-Go Fun Box
Stock a box or bin with fun things to take on an outing or a trip: a kite, binoculars, a bird book, bubbles, a ball, and a Frisbee. When you're heading out, you can grab a few things from the box or keep the whole thing in your car.

The Party Bucket
Stock an ice or beverage bucket with fun things for a spontaneous party: board games, playing cards and a book of card games, party cups, plates, napkins, candles, sparklers, and CDs with music suitable for different kinds of parties.

The Swagger Wagon
If you have room in the trunk of your car for a couple of beach chairs and a beach bag with bathing suits, towels, blanket, magazines, a few beach toys, and sunscreen, then you're all ready for a spontaneous beach or park stop.

glow-in-the-dark bracelets and necklaces, a cocktail recipe book, hot dog forks, and s'mores supplies.

A friend of mine set up a bin for camping entertainment: dice and card games, a knot-tying book, light-up yo-yos, a magnifying glass and bug vacuum, bird and mammal guides, a how to juggle book, and more. These were things she had lying around her house that were not being used. Put into the camping bin, though, they were a huge hit. Whenever she runs across other things that she thinks will be fun for camping, she tosses them in to keep the entertainment fresh.

Organizing these seldom used items can also help clear things out of other areas of your house, where they can't easily be found or aren't being used. Who knows what will wind up in your party bucket or fun box? It may bring new life to something that's unused and been kicking around your house for years.

Whether you're a Planner or an NSMP, enjoy planning your summer fun. Who knows where the wind will take you!

Action Plan

- Create "Fun Files."
- Stock an on-the-go fun box and a party bucket.
- Put some useful and fun things in your car as well as items that will keep you comfortable during last-minute stops.

Reaping What You Sow
Wendy Lomme, Landscape Designer

"It was a soft, reposeful summer landscape, as lovely as a dream,
and as lonesome as Sunday."
— *Mark Twain*

My favorite part of summer is being able to walk around barefoot. I'll just tell it like it is. Up until recently, like the cobbler without any shoes, I was the landscaper without a garden. It wasn't a lack of desire by any means, just a lack of time as I was building and running a young company. I, of course, spent plenty of time working in other people's gardens, talking about plants, and daydreaming of my future garden.

This spring I found myself with an abundance of unsellable large planting pots, and after two months of thinking about it, I finally planted my own veggie garden! My yard may still be full of misfit plants, and I might not water everything as much as I should, but in a few weeks, I'll at least be able to snack on a few fresh cherry tomatoes and crisp cucumbers from my repurposed planting pots. I'll probably still be barefoot, and happy as can be!

Summer is actually a little polarizing: on one hand, the warm weather and long days are motivation to be active. On the other hand, the heat and out-of-school mentality can lead to lazy days. Nature expresses the same duality, in that plant life is at its "peak" this season, but most processes slow or stop in order to conserve energy. If we take a cue from nature, we can embrace the sedentary and enjoy the abundance of the season.

Your Outdoor Living Room

In recent years, a movement has spread to use our yards as outdoor living space. Some yards have separate "rooms," with areas for cooking, entertaining, reading, and so on. Some yards have full outdoor kitchens with running water, lighting, and stone ovens. No matter the scale, the result is the same: a functional space that adds value to your property and, more importantly, a reason to be outside. Here are a few key ideas to bring your living room out to your yard:

Vertical space The right vertical accents make a small space feel big, or a large area feel nice and cozy. Not everyone can afford to have a full wooden or metal pergola or an arbor system installed in the yard. But how about four large metal or bamboo stakes with a string of lights extended between them? How about a few large pots with a trellis and vine in each, to create some privacy? One of my clients wanted just a little more privacy between her and her townhome neighbor. Our simple fix was to add an arbor along the top of the wooden fence and plant two vines at either end to fill in and add some texture, fragrance, and green screen.

Floor space Natural stone can add a very warm and organic touch to an outdoor space. Flagstone can be installed directly into dirt, with groundcover growing between the stones. Or, if you have a patio space and want to liven it up, try an outdoor rug to add color and texture. It will survive the summer rains, and can easily be cleaned and rolled up for winter storage.

Furniture Do you love to "escape" from your house by yourself to read a book with a glass of wine? Then make sure your outdoor living room has seating only for one! Try a hammock or papasan chair. Or create a cozy, casual patio space for a quiet retreat with room for just you (no husbands or children allowed!). Perhaps you are a social butterfly, hosting a new group of friends each weekend? Offer a variety of seating to suit all of your guests, old and young alike: folding or beach chairs found at a thrift store, oversize pillows to pop-a-squat on the ground, and tall stools that stack and take up little space.

Victory Gardens

Check out this still pertinent excerpt from *The Facts About 1945 Victory Gardens*, a flyer distributed by the U.S. government during World War II.

1. **Garden for victory.** Gardens that supply 40 percent of our fresh vegetables are essential to win the war.
2. **Grow your own and play safe.** If you have your own fruits and vegetables, you don't have to worry about crop failures in other parts of the country.
3. **Save money.**
4. **Build your health.** There's nothing like exercise and better meals to improve your health.
5. **Homegrown food is tastier.**
6. **Gardening is fun.** It makes you feel good. It relaxes your nerves. It's a family enterprise that brings together father and mother, son and daughter.
7. **Gardens help the community.** [They] promote neighborliness, sociability, and cooperation.

Your Outdoor Farmers' Market

We all know that things go in cycles—heck, I just saw a "young adult" wearing a bright green fluorescent hat and fluorescent pink sunglasses, which is one trend I really hoped wouldn't return! Alas, the recurrence of some trends, such as homegrown food, is better than others. As with the victory gardens of the early to mid-1900s, people today are digging in and getting dirty. The motivation has shifted slightly, though. The victory gardens were in response to produce shortages during World Wars I and II, and were viewed as a patriotic duty and a way to support the troops. The recurrence of the trend these days has more to do with healthy food and a cost-effective way to eat organically. Some benefits of homegrown food:

- It is cost-effective.
- It is more nutritious, with greater amounts of trace minerals.
- It reduces your carbon footprint, bypassing the ecological costs of shipping.
- It retains nutrient content. It's always best to eat as soon as possible after harvesting!
- Gardening is cool!
- It is educational for children and adults.

Spreading the Love (with Fruit)

Do you have one too many apple trees in your yard? Do you see your neighbors' cherries and plums going to waste? Consider putting that food to good use. Check out cityfruit.org or look for similar organizations in your neighborhood or city. They collect homegrown fruit to distribute to food banks, meal programs, senior centers, schools, and others who can use it.

Action Plan

For the Urban Dweller:

You may have minimal space, but anyone can grow some fresh herbs and veggies if you have a sunny 5' x 5' balcony or even just a window-sill. Here are some tips and tricks:

- When purchasing decorative pots, go for the biggest size(s) that will fit your space. More soil = more water retention = happier plants (and you).

- Use pots of varying sizes to create a trio or cluster. This will add dimension and interest to the space.

- One key to successful herbs and veggies is water! Consider installing a simple drip system with a timer to do the watering for you.

- Worried about water rings? If your pots are indoors, or above your neighbor's balcony, plant directly into a nursery pot and place the nursery pot inside a decorative pot that does not contain a drainage hole.

For the Garden Gal:

The lazy days of summer don't necessarily apply to the garden! At least we can tan while we work. Here are some tips and tricks:

- Veggies prefer morning drinks, while ornamentals and lawns typically prefer evening drinks. Cheers!
- Check your plant stakes/strings/propping devices and adjust them to accommodate your growing plants.
- Harvest, harvest, harvest! It's best to pick ripe veggies often to encourage successive production and to achieve the best flavor.
- Create a plot plan and start prepping beds for fall planting.

Chapter 3
Fall
Completing the Incompletes

"No spring nor summer beauty hath such grace,
as I have seen in one autumnal face."
—*John Donne*

Fall has a beauty all its own. As the earth slows down and plants and trees shed their leaves, we get to enjoy one final display of brilliant color, like nature's fireworks. The wildlife is busy nesting, settling in for the colder weather to come. Harvesting and gathering take the form of picking edibles, raking leaves, and tidying up.

With fall comes a new focus. It's a time to scrapbook and Pinterest the pictures of summer and step back into a more sustainable, yummy pace of life. Like the trees, it's time to shed the old and reorganize our lives to prepare for winter.

In fall you will:

- Do away with energy drains for good.
- Restore your body's balance.
- Become the household diva of papers, schedules, stuff, oh my!
- Reconnect with nature.

Taking Care of the Leaky Bucket

Chieko Watanabe, Life Coach

"If you don't like something, change it; if you can't change it,
change the way you think about it. "
—*Mary Engelbreit*

There's that first evening that inevitably comes around with a chill in the air that tells me it's time to replace my light summer quilt and take out my heavy down comforter to keep me warm through the night. Shortly after, the leaves start to turn and the hillsides look like they are on fire with bright yellow, orange, and red leaves, and before you know it, the trees have shed themselves for winter. Fall is a time when we say goodbye to the chaos of summer and reground ourselves to a quieter rhythm and structure.

Completing the Incompletes

Before any major transition, it's great to shed past lingering "stuff" I call the Incompletes. These are tasks, projects, relationships, and ideas that are incomplete and just hanging out there somewhere on your to-do list.

This spring I folded a thousand cranes in the Japanese tradition in hopes of fully resolving some health issues. It took many hours and I folded until my fingers were sore. The great news is I finished all one thousand cranes! However, as summer started, I lost focus and did not take the next step of sewing the cranes together. I still cannot hang them as an installation piece in my home to continually bless me with good health. So the cranes remain in a box in the closet—an Incomplete.

The problem with the Incompletes is that they hold us back. We feel guilty when we are reminded of our Incompletes, and they take up space mentally and energetically, and in my case of the one thousand cranes, physically too. As with many of our Incompletes, the amount of time and energy to take this project to full completion is often minimal. I need two additional supplies from the craft store and a couple of hours to string them all together for the installation. It seems so simple, yet I pushed it off all summer and it's consistently nagged at me.

As we step into fall, I will take on this Incomplete and spend the extra time and effort to bring it to 100 percent completion. Ahhh . . . it immediately replaces my feelings of guilt with a sense of accomplishment, satisfaction, and even a boost in self-esteem. I am no longer "The girl who starts a bunch of projects and finishes none." Now I am, "The girl who diligently works until the job is 100 percent done!" That feels so much better. I've cleared up the storage space that the cranes were taking in the closet and now have a beautiful, unique, handmade installation.

Take a look around your house, desk, computer files, garden, and even your contact list to see what Incompletes are lurking. Is there a phone call you need to make? Is there a care package you need to take to the post office? You let go of the energy they hold over you by completing these tasks. While they may seem insignificant individually, don't underestimate their impact. The cumulative energy of the many small

Incompletes—and the duration for which you carry them—becomes a heavy burden.

When my clients take on the assignment of completing their Incompletes, they inevitability say, "Wow, I feel so much lighter! I didn't realize how much these things sucked my energy!" Chances are, your Incompletes are making you feel guilty and taking a lot more time and energy than you may realize.

There's a Hole in Your Bucket, Dear Liza

There are days when life just feels draining, like you've sprung a serious leak in your energy tank. There may be one big leak, such as a death in the family, or a move that's sucking all your energy like a vampire. It's more often that you will have many small leaks from various little things in life when you are losing energy almost imperceptibly. Just like a bucket with many small holes, you can lose a lot of energy fast if you don't take the time to plug these leaks.

We tolerate a lot in life. I've tolerated many things: a home where I had to walk through muddy grass to get from my car to the front door every day, shoes that just didn't quite fit right, a slow Internet connection, eating poorly, sleep deprivation, a disorganized hall closet, bad lighting, a dirty car, faulty light switches, a shortage of coffee tumblers. I've tolerated less than ideal relationships: jealousy from a friend who couldn't be happy for me, negativity from my family, clients who aren't a good fit. You can see how these lists could go on and on. You probably have a similar list: a door that doesn't shut property, a slow computer, lost sunglasses, broken appliances, and so on. Think through your home, garden, and desk, the people in your life, and even your own behavior and you'll probably find dozens more.

Now imagine that each one of these things you are tolerating is a small leak in your energy tank. That burnt-out light bulb that needs to be replaced takes your energy every time you try to turn it on and you are reminded that you need to go to the store and get a new light bulb. It takes mental space to try to remember, and emotional space due to continually feeling badly for not having taken care of it already. Just like the Incompletes,

Things We Tolerate

- Broken appliances
- A dirty house
- A messy garage
- Itchy clothes
- Disorganized desks
- Dirty windows
- Long commutes
- Toxic people
- Self-criticism
- Junk food
- An uncomfortable bed
- Unpaid bills
- Broken jewelry
- Ugly furniture
- Unfinished projects
- Lack of sleep
- Back pain
- Bad hair
- Being tired
- Bad habits

each toleration may be small, but the cumulative effect is exhausting.

So what can you do? You can plug these energy drains one at a time by zapping these tolerations. Go out and wash the car that makes you feel embarrassed every time you drive it around. Stop by the store and get the light bulb you need and replace it. Call on your handy person to help you take care of the broken things around the house that need repair. Immediately, you'll feel a shift in your energy!

Make it a fun game and see how many tolerations you can zap each day or week. I had a client who made it a competition between her and her partner to see who could get to 50 zapped tolerations first. The result? One hundred tolerations between them taken care of in their home and their lives. It's amazing how these simple little things can add up to restore energy and give you a sense of satisfaction and happiness. Next time you go out to your car, it will be sparkling clean and make you smile. Next time you turn on the light, it will illuminate the room and your heart. Next time you open your organized hall closet, you'll be able to easily find your dustpan and feel accomplished. That's the power of zapping tolerations.

Grounding to Peace and Purpose

With your Incompletes completed and tolerations zapped, you enter a calm state of mind where you can refocus and get back to what's truly important. This is a great time to be reminded of your purpose. What's really important here? What are you here to do?

These are big questions and they should be asked often. If nothing comes up for you, don't worry. It doesn't mean that you don't have a purpose. It just means that you are less connected to it and the answer isn't as accessible. These questions aren't necessarily about what you do for work (though it can be), and they don't have to require dramatic life changes, such as backpacking around the globe for two years. Fall is about getting clear on what's most important to you in life and reconnecting with those elements.

Sometimes my clients are looking for a certain kind of answer, such as, "My life purpose is to help children in Africa affected by malaria," or, "My life purpose is to be a painter." The truth is, our life purpose has more to do with intention than it does with modality of execution. My life purpose is to help people build confidence. I could deliver on this mission through many different channels: as a therapist, fashion consultant, personal trainer, hairdresser, plastic surgeon, or designer of slimming jeans. But I chose to become a coach, writer, and speaker specializing in helping clients create amazing lives with heart-based businesses.

Action Plan

Begin with the Little Stuff Although it may seem counterintuitive to start with things such as tolerations and incompletes, it's what is really necessary to create the space in your mind and space in your heart to ask these bigger questions. By stripping away the noise, you can be left with the essential. Only after creating a quiet and peaceful place should such questions be asked, because your inner guide only whispers.

Set the Intention When you reconnect with your purpose, your heart begins to open, and it's a great place to start setting intentions, plans, and strategies for fall. What do I need to focus on right now? What do I WANT to focus on right now?

Detoxing without Dieting

Michelle Babb, MS, RD, Nutritionist

"Eat food, not too much, mostly plants."
—*Michael Pollan*

Before I became a foodie, I was much less enthusiastic about the arrival of fall. Being the sun-worshiping summer girl that I am, I always considered autumn to be a pesky precursor to winter. Once I started studying nutrition at Bastyr University, where the emphasis is on eating local, organic, whole foods, I realized that the early months of fall produce the greatest variety of vegetables. In fact, some of the most nutritious foods that nature has to offer make their appearance in September and October, including beets, hearty greens, apples, pears, pumpkins, and other types of squash packed with beta-carotene. Let the feasting begin!

Post-Summer Cleanup

Clients often confess that September brings some relief from the unpredictability and unstructured nature of summer. The kids are back in school, vacation time has run out, and it's time to reestablish regular routines. It's not surprising that fall has become prime season for nutritional cleansing or "detox" programs. This is actually my favorite time to guide my clients through a nutritional cleanse. Fresh produce is still abundant, with a wide variety of fruits and vegetables, and a 21-day cleanse is the perfect way to hit the reset button. It's also a great way to lay the foundation for healthier eating patterns during the impending holiday season.

When I hear the words "detox diet" I can't help but cringe, knowing there's an entire industry built around the concept of purging the body of "toxic" substances. I've had clients proudly profess they have gone on semi-starvation diets, fasts, or a certain type of "cleanse" consisting of lemon juice, maple syrup, and cayenne pepper. These clients are often fueled by a desperate desire for rapid weight loss. "And it really worked," they'll exclaim, "for a while . . ."

Tips for the Sensible Detoxer

- Take a break from caffeine and alcohol.
- Avoid refined sugar and artificial sweeteners (sucrose, evaporated cane juice, high-fructose corn syrup, aspartame, sucralose, etc.).
- Drink plenty of water and/or herbal tea (minimum of 2 liters per day).
- Experiment with cutting out dairy and gluten.
- Eat lots of fresh fruits and vegetables, legumes, whole grains, nuts, seeds, and wild-caught fish.
- Read labels and avoid unfamiliar ingredients.

Here's what desperate detoxers often don't know: our liver is the gatekeeper and bouncer for unwanted substances in the body, and it relies on a whole army of nutrients to be able to sift, sort, and purge toxins. In other words, starving yourself to rid your body of toxins could be disabling the army and doing more harm than good. It goes without saying that rapid weight loss is ALWAYS followed by an unwelcome return of the weight, along with a few new pounds that tag along for the ride.

This is why I ask that all of my clients who embark on the 21-day nutritional cleanse do so with a goal of restoring balance to the body and discovering healthy, intuitive eating patterns that can be sustained well beyond the cleanse. I make it known that this is not to be treated as a "Hollywood cleanse," where you mind your Ps and Qs for a few weeks to shed some pounds and then resume the same habits that made you feel off-kilter in the first place. A nutritional cleanse, done properly, is about honoring the body and nourishing it in a way that supports optimal function and holistic wellness.

Perhaps that seems like an ominous task, particularly if you are a chronic dieter and/or have a dysfunctional relationship with food. In fact, there are people I discourage from doing a cleanse, such as those who have a history of anorexia and those who are hyper-focused on food restriction. Others can improve their relationship with food by focusing on eating more of the foods that support good nutrition, such as vegetables, fruit, legumes, whole grains, nuts, seeds, fish and other lean proteins, and healthy fats and oils. There's no calorie counting or obsessing over grams of fat and protein, and carbs are not considered evil. It's just about eating well and tuning in to the innate wisdom of the body.

Listen to Your Body Language

If spring is a time of emergence, then fall is a time of introspection and inward focus. Again, we could take our cues from nature and agriculture, where fall is the time to reap the benefits we've sowed over the spring and summer. It's when we enjoy the harvest and celebrate abundance, and then we begin our preparation for the more dormant months that lie ahead. It's the perfect time to establish healthy patterns (before the holidays hit) and take comfort in routine.

Notice that your body starts to crave different types of food as the season changes. You might start to gravitate toward starchier root vegetables and warming foods as you become less interested in salads and lighter dishes. Honor that preference and make it easier on yourself by shopping for foods that are in season. It's a great time to start experimenting with soup recipes and roasting big trays of veggies to snack on through the week.

Favorite Fall Foods for Cleansing

Whether you're toying with the idea of doing a full-blown nutritional cleanse or you just want to do some cleanup work after all the summer events, barbecues, and social gatherings, the following foods are the perfect addition to your diet.

1. **Broccoli.** This hearty, cruciferous vegetable stands out as one of the most nutrient-rich foods you can

Nutrition Speak

Antioxidants substances found in foods like fruits and vegetables that destroy damaging free radicals in the body.

Cruciferous vegetables vegetables that are in the cabbage family, including broccoli, cauliflower, kale, Brussels sprouts, and bok choy. This family of veggies is best known for its cancer-fighting phytonutrients.

Indole-3-carbinol a powerful compound found in cruciferous vegetables that has hormone-balancing and cancer-preventing effects in the body.

Inulin a specific type of dietary fiber found in bananas, onions, leeks, and sunchokes. Useful for lowering cholesterol and managing blood sugar.

Phenols powerful antioxidants found in berries, greens, whole grains, and legumes.

Phytonutrients natural chemicals found in plants that protect them from environmental insults. These protective nutrients also offer health benefits to those who eat high-phytonutrient foods.

Tubers a category of vegetables with a "swollen stem" that grows underground. Potatoes, yams, and jicama fit into this category of plants.

eat. Not only is it packed with antioxidants that help prevent cancer and heart disease, but it also contains specific phytonutrients that support the two phases of liver detoxification. It's great sautéed with mushrooms, onions, and red peppers.

2. **Beets.** What's not to love about beets? I believe they're nature's perfect food. The same compounds that give them their beautiful reddish purple color make them a power food that provides anti-inflammatory, antioxidant, and detox benefits. Shred them on a salad to keep all those great nutrients intact, or try them roasted and finished with a dash of balsamic vinegar.

3. **Pears.** This lovely fall fruit is often overlooked and should be getting more credit for being a phenomenal source of fiber and a rich source of nutrients. Pears have been gaining a bit more attention because of their unique phenolic compounds. The flavonoids in the skin of the pear are potent antioxidants that also provide anti-inflammatory benefits. Snack on pears with walnuts and feta, or try them baked for a simple, delicious dessert.

4. **Brussels sprouts.** If you're turning up your nose at Brussels sprouts because you had a bad steam-table version that was cooked beyond recognition, then it's time to try these little treasures again. Brussels sprouts are in the cruciferous vegetable family and most of their notoriety comes from studies that have shown cancer-fighting benefits. They also contain a specific compound called indole-3-carbinol that helps the body metabolize estrogen into its more protective form and can be good for healthy hormone balance. To roast Brussels sprouts, toss them in a liberal amount of grapeseed or sunflower oil,

add sea salt, spread on a roasting pan, and bake at 375°F for about 20 minutes, or until soft but not soggy.

5. **Sunchokes (Jerusalem artichokes).** This sweet little tuber is knobby like ginger but slightly larger and plumper. Sunchokes are a superior source of inulin, a dietary fiber that acts as a prebiotic, so it helps feed the good bacteria (probiotics) in the gut. It's also great for blood sugar management. Sunchokes contain B vitamins, potassium, calcium, and magnesium. They're great shredded on a salad, sautéed, or roasted. I like to roast them with celery root and then blend with vegetable broth to make an easy, creamy soup.

Ride It Out: Enjoy the Payoff!

When you're experimenting with a nutritional cleanse, notice what messages your body is sending. You might feel fatigued and irritable in the first week as your body withdraws from caffeine, sugar, and alcohol and begins to detox. Severe sugar cravings may dissipate after a few days of avoiding refined sugar and moods start to stabilize. Often sleep quality improves, and you can wake easily without the promise of caffeine.

Action Plan

Try a nutritional cleanse and establish an ongoing routine that supports healthy, intuitive eating.

- Make a commitment to avoid caffeine, sugar, and alcohol for three to four weeks.

- Focus on eating five small meals a day.
- Eat mostly vegetables, fruit, whole grains (like quinoa and brown rice), beans, nuts, seeds, and fish.
- Avoid processed foods.
- Drink at least two liters of water every day.
- Keep a diary to track how you're feeling physically, mentally, and emotionally through the course of the cleanse.

Wrangling Your Wayward Macaroni

Karen Pfeiffer Bush, Professional Organizer

"Don't you love the Fall? I would send you a bouquet of newly sharpened pencils if I knew your name and address."
—*Nora Ephron*

Fall is collection time. It's when we evaluate the nest to determine its stores and condition before we settle in for winter. We collect and compile the flashes of ideas and dreams sprouted during the invigorating summer. It's a time to gather supplies needed for the new school year and embark on new systems, new ventures, new roles, and so on. Board meetings start up again after a summer break. Sports teams and clubs distribute calendars and phone lists. Like busy squirrels collecting nuts to store for winter, we scurry around collecting schedules, supplies, and hopefully our thoughts and goals.

For many, it's a time of new beginnings and fresh starts. It's also a time to regain balance. Around the autumnal equinox, when the day and nighttime hours are equal, many people, consciously or not, assess and seek balance in their homes and lives.

Professional organizers receive many new client phone calls in the fall. The chaos of summer has passed and suddenly people look around their homes at the things they've avoided by remaining outside or on the go for much of the summer. For some, this can be a time of anxiety when they realize what they've left undone while they were having their summer fun.

The autumn light is softer and gentler but allows us to see a little better than in the bright, hot light of summer. I am a summer girl, but I can definitely see more clearly in the fall. I've never lost the student mind-set that fall is an exciting time filled with new things: a time to regroup and "rein it all in."

For those of us who are teachers, students, or parents of students, the focus of fall is back to school: textbooks and school supplies, new "looks," bus schedules, new shoes and clothes, uniforms, lunch boxes, instruments, sports gear, medical releases, class schedules, locker combinations, reams and reams and reams of PAPER. Anyone aside from me feel like she's going to hyperventilate right now? Breathe in through the nose, out through the mouth. It's going to be okay!

New schedules and the beginning of the school year often go hand in hand with chaos. Piles of paper, gear, and supplies seem to multiply on their own at the front or back door, kitchen counter, or dining room table. If you can stand it, this is an excellent time to sit back and be an observer. Where do those backpacks get dropped? Where do the papers get deposited and the shoes get tossed? See if you can live with it for a bit. Pay attention to the patterns. You may have adorable hooks on the wall with each household member's name on it, but do the jackets or backpacks actually wind up there? Repairing broken-down organizational systems sometimes requires habit development or training. However, it's often a reflection of the fact that the systems are not easy enough.

When creating zones and systems in your home, keep in mind the animals, and I don't mean your family members. I'm referring to animals in the wild. They typically nest near their feeding grounds and have everything they need close by. Focus on what's natural and intuitive. If schoolwork happens at the kitchen counter, create a storage space nearby for the supplies that are necessary for your little animals to do their work. If jackets don't wind up on the hooks, maybe the hooks are placed too high or too low.

Kid Paper: The Sad Story of Loose Macaroni and Wayward Pools of Glitter

In my tours through the depths of collected kid art and papers, I have seen many a sad-looking macaroni floating in a wayward pool of glitter in the bottom of a box stored deep in someone's basement. Let me ask you this: is that box filled with wrinkled artwork and school papers bringing joy to anyone deep in the recesses of the basement? My answer, and hopefully yours, is, "Nope!" Oh, to think of all the macaroni that has met its demise in a glittery sea of loneliness. Unbearable!

Don't get me wrong. I am as sentimental as the next mom and get a kick out of the creations that come home in the backpack. Why shove them into a box to be enjoyed later? When? And by whom? And IF that time ever comes, will there be anything left to be enjoyed?

The point is, if you're keeping kid art and schoolwork because it's special, then treat it as such. I know your little darlings are complete artistic and scholarly geniuses, but in the case of keeping their creations, the age-old adage "Less is more" rings especially true.

A Coffee Table Book for Your Little *Artiste*

Here is a system that will not only preserve the precious art and schoolwork but also act as a scheduling and contact management tool throughout the school year.

1. Create a binder for each kid for each school year.
2. Get a three-ring binder and fill it with sheet protectors.
3. Add dividers labeled "Schedules," "Contacts," and "Keepers," with several sheet protectors in each section.
4. You may choose to have other sections as well for "Sports," "Afterschool Activities," "Reading Calendars," "Chores," or "Wish Lists" for holidays or birthdays.
5. In the Keepers section, add dividers for each month of the school year.
6. You and your little artiste decide together how many sheet protectors there should be per month. Keep in mind that you want your binder to be able to close flat, so probably no more than six sheet protectors per month.

Coffee Table Book

When those creations come home, work with your little geniuses to figure out which ones are worthy of the Coffee Table Book and slip the special ones into the sheet protectors for that month. If they find they're out of sheet protectors, they'll need to decide which one gets cut from the book.

Keep some addressed and posted envelopes in or near the binder so the pieces that get cut from the book can be dropped into an envelope with a little note and mailed to grandparents, friends, or other relatives. Or snap a digital photo of the art or school paper and email it.

When I first introduce the Coffee Table Book to kids, I ask them if they've ever seen one. I explain that there are coffee table books of Ansel Adams, Renoir, and even Leonardo da Vinci that feature a particular period of their lives and work. If those books held every piece of art they ever created, it would be too big and no one could appreciate it all. Only the most special pieces of their art from that period can be featured in the book. This allows the collection to be truly enjoyed and appreciated.

More Than Just Artwork

Your children's schedules, reading lists, and phone trees tell the story of their lives as much as their masterpieces do. Keep current calendars, phone lists, and other reference materials in the front of the binder. This way, everyone in the family (hopefully my husband is reading this) will go to the binder to see when the basketball game is, instead of calling Mom, "The Keeper of All Information," while she's at work.

At the end of the school year, you'll have a great snapshot of what life was like for your artistic and scholarly genius when he was in first grade. He created his first Coffee Table Book! Imagine the nostalgic value of having twelve beautiful Coffee Table Books on display, as opposed to forgotten boxes in the recesses of the basement. Now that's special!

Household Binder

The binder system is not just a tool for kids. Family or household binders are also a great way to store regularly needed information that's relevant to running the household. This could include a section with contact information for plumbers, housecleaners, doctors, and so on. You can have sections for restaurant menus; coupons and gift certificates; membership cards; and instructions for babysitters, house sitters, and pet sitters. Keeping regularly needed information all in one place cuts down on searching through individual files or databases.

This may seem like a lot of work up front, but the benefit is, it frees "The Keeper of All Information" from being interrupted at happy hour. I mean work.

Action Plan

Create a Coffee Table Book for each child and/or a household binder.

Create a To-Do Box, a Going Out Box, and a Donation Station.

With the onset of new routines comes a lot of in and out. People and their things come in and people and their things go out. Creating in- and outboxes is a great way to corral the chaos. Chieko addresses the Incompletes. She coaches clients through identifying those Incompletes and checking them off the list. In- and outboxes are temporary storage for the physical items that are necessary to complete the Incompletes.

- **To-Do Box** Create a To-Do Box for non-paper items. Perhaps you have a sweater that needs a new button or a CD to transfer to your iPod. Put them in your To-Do Box and add the task to your list. When you've got time for mending or downloading, you'll know right where to go to find the item associated with the task.

- **Going Out Box** Put your packages that need to be taken to the post office, the library books that need to be returned, the light bulb that needs to be replaced in a Going Out Box. Schedule errands in your calendar and when it's errand time, go to your Going Out Box to get the items that are needed to complete the

Incompletes. You will save precious time by avoiding the great treasure hunt for the special battery or paint swatch that you know you set aside for when you finally had time to hit the hardware store. A key to the success of the To-Do Box or Going Out Box is to make sure that you have backed up those physical items either on a list or in your calendar. Some people like to post the To-Do Lists near their To-Do or Going Out Box. Others prefer to create reminders or tasks in a planner or calendar. Items that are not used, loved, or have a task associated with them are CLUTTER—the physical version of Incompletes.

- **Donation Station** Designate and label a box for donations. Whenever you identify something from around the house that is no longer loved, used, or needed, put it in the Donation Station. When it's full, take it right out to the car and deliver it to a donation site the next time you're out and about.

Appreciating Beauty in Transition
Wendy Lomme, Landscape Designer

October gave a party;
The leaves by hundreds came—
The Chestnuts, Oaks, and Maples,
And leaves of every name.
The Sunshine spread a carpet,
And everything was grand,
Miss Weather led the dancing,
Professor Wind, the band.
—*George Cooper, "October's Party"*

I was fortunate enough as a child to take dance classes for nine years. I loved everything about it—the teachers, my classmates, the discipline, and most of all, the costumes. The dance company held recitals each fall, where each and every class had the opportunity to perform and showcase the results of our hard work. The backstage was a flurry of excitement. The teachers and family helped with hair, makeup, and, in my case, three or four costume changes. When the time was right, we stepped onto the stage, bathed in the warm spotlights, and showed off our brilliant costumes and (hopefully) awesome dance moves.

As a season, fall embodies the same excitement and brilliant display as my dance recitals did. It is the "other spring," offering new beginnings and a subtle transition to a bolder season. There is a lot of excitement at the beginning of the season—squeezing in the last outdoor activities, heading back to school, and packing away summer gear. In the landscape, there is the same flurry of activity—perennials are producing their last blooms, fruits and veggies are ready for harvesting, and the parched soil is being replenished with warm rains.

Harvesting > Thanking > Giving

The excitement of fall historically centers on harvesting the abundant summer crops. For me, that translates to plucking the last ripe tomato, snipping fresh herbs for drying, and squeezing the winter squashes to see whether they are ready for the pantry. Whether you grow vegetables or not, you can no doubt enjoy the next phase of harvesting: eating and celebrating! Thanksgiving kicks off the holiday season with a delicious feast and time enjoyed with family and friends. There are many similar traditions and holidays celebrated around the world that feature giving thanks for food and sharing the abundance with family, neighbors, and those less fortunate.

If you venture to grow your own food, you may experience a personal "bumper crop" in the form of several pounds of tomatoes or a few dozen zucchini. A great idea is to trade some of your crop with neighbors or friends who have too many potatoes or green beans to eat. If you have extra space in your garden, consider intentionally growing extras to bring to your local food bank.

You may also experience some "extras" in your garden beds or pots. If your plants are happy and healthy, they may over time outgrow the original spot where they were planted. For many perennials and bulbs, you have the option to divide and share:

- Dig up the plant you would like to divide.
- Break the plant in half or into multiple sections.
- Use a sharp spade or handsaw to navigate the roots.
- Replant what you want to keep, adding a topdressing of compost.
- Give away the other pieces of the plant and make someone smile!

Beauty in Transition

One of my favorite trees to watch during the fall season is the katsura (*Cercidiphyllum japonica*). It is a fantastic midsize tree that is perfect as a featured tree in your garden or planted in the parking strip along the street. During the fall, the heart-shaped leaves turn from green to brilliant yellow and orange. The tree isn't done yet. As the leaves fall to the ground they smell of burnt sugar, appealing to your olfactory as well as visual senses.

Let's don our five-year-old curiosity caps, and ask, "Why do leaves change color?" "Why do trees and shrubs drop leaves in the fall?" It's all about energy! The plants have been actively building their food supply throughout the summer months, as they know weaker sunlight and shorter days are coming. They simply aren't able to produce enough food to survive the winter, so they start prioritizing.

The purpose of leaves is to collect water and sunlight to produce food, a.k.a. chlorophyll, for the tree or plant. Once the supply is full, the leaves become extraneous. The trees and shrubs wisely let them die. As they die, the chlorophyll is drained from the leaves, leaving behind brilliant reds, oranges, purples, and yellows. The tree is left to rest for the season, awaiting new growth in the spring.

My grandma loved to preserve beauty. She taught me to search for small treasures: a pretty flower, a lucky four-leaf clover, and brilliant-colored leaves. In the fall, we would look for leaves big and small to preserve. We would press the leaves in between sheets of wax paper and then iron them. After that, the preserved beauties would live on the bookshelf tucked between pages, ready to be discovered by the next reader.

We have the pleasure of enjoying the brilliant fall colors and the opportunity to mimic the trees in the fall. It's a great time of year to shed the unnecessary and unwanted. With shorter days, we hibernate in our own way with more time indoors and lower energy levels. This is our chance to rest and reflect, preparing for the cold winter.

Even though the trees don't want their leaves, we can still use them—and not just for making big piles to jump in. Use the leaves to start a compost pile or add to your composting bin. They can be placed in garden beds, acting as a layer of mulch to suppress weed growth. You can also mow right over them and let the clippings and shredded leaves stay on the lawn. Over the winter, the wet leaves will break down, adding nutrients to your beds and lawn.

A Tree to Hug

Fall is also a fantastic time of year to plant a new tree. If you have room in your yard, consider adding a quality that might be missing from your garden: fall color, interesting winter bark, spring blooms, shade in the

Plant Your Love

I've had the honor and pleasure of meeting many special plants and trees through my line of work. It touches my heart to hear a client say, "This hydrangea is special to me. My best friend gave it to me in honor of my father's passing." What an amazing way to remember a loved one!

For me, it's a brilliant, purple-flowered azalea that I planted when I lost my beloved grandma. Purple is our favorite color, and each spring it brings me such joy to watch it leaf out, then bud, then bloom; it gives me a reason to slow down and remember how precious life is.

For my mom, it's an almost 100-year-old grapefruit tree (potted and kept indoors, except in the summer) that her mother grew and nourished. In the years since I've known the tree, it has been brought back from the brink of death, had various diseases, and even served as our Christmas tree (yup, Charlie Brown style!). A special plant or tree is a fantastic way to honor a loved one through the generations.

heat of summer. If there isn't room near your house, perhaps you have an empty parking strip between the road and sidewalk. Many areas offer street tree programs to promote the planting of new trees in a safe and effective manner. After all, trees add property value and clean the air for us.

If neither of these options works for you, check out local groups that organize park restoration projects and head on down to pitch in. Chances are, there are some invasive plant species that need removing. Once an area is cleared, the parks department often plants native shrubs and trees to outcompete the invasive species. This is a great way to have an impact locally and globally.

Settling In

By the end of fall, a calm has settled over the great outdoors. The bare branches and muted colors mean that most of the work is done for the season. In warm, rainy climates like the Pacific Northwest, this is the best time to plant and transplant. It gives the opportunity for the plants and trees to settle in through the winter, establish some roots, and take advantage of the free water for the next six months or so.

Fall is also an ideal time of year for pruning most trees and shrubs. Nature actually leads the way and takes care of some of this work for us, with strong winds, ice, or snow relieving the trees of weak or dead branches. You can finish the job by eliminating unhealthy and crossing branches through pruning, which will provide better air circulation. This allows the plant life to approach the spring lighter, fitter, and better able to focus on growing healthy and strong.

If you're envisioning yourself as Edward Scissorhands, drop your weapon. Please, no topiary menagerie. Remember, nature is not to be controlled but rather encouraged and supported for all to enjoy.

Got Grass?

With a little time, cheap or free materials, and some patience, you can get rid of your unwanted grass and at the same time condition the soil for a garden bed by sheet mulching. This involves building layers of materials that smother the grass and break down over time. The first layer placed directly on the grass is thick cardboard or many layers of newspaper. Fallen leaves and green clippings (non-woody material) are perfect for the next layer. The top layer can be bark chips, mulch, or arborist chips, which you can often get for free from tree companies or the parks department. With the fall and winter rains, the layers will decompose, successfully eradicating the grass and leaving a new bed ready for planting!

Got Water?

Set up your water catchment system so that you don't run into trouble with standing water and flooding in the middle of winter. Here are two options for dealing with too much water:

- Cisterns, the big mama of rain barrels, are large holding tanks for rainwater. There are several companies making creative cisterns to live snug up against houses, under decks, or even between fences. Cisterns provide free water to use in your garden in the middle of the summer.
- Raingardens are sunken gardens that catch and filter water. The purpose of the raingarden is threefold:
    1. It's a place to direct extra water on your property.
    2. It slows the deluge of water that can flood street drains in the winter.
    3. It cleans the water (thank you, plants!) before it makes its way to our rivers and oceans.

Action Plan

Feeling Easy-Peasy Walk through your neighborhood or favorite park and find your favorite fall color. Take a picture or a small memento (a leaf or an already broken branch) to display and enjoy every day. If you're extra inspired, see if you can bring that color into your yard (your local nursery can help you identify what it is) or into your home (New paint? Accent pillows? Coffee mugs?).

Weekend Warrior Get into the giving spirit. Peruse your yard for overgrown perennials and start dividing. Wrap the new "baby" plants in burlap and tie them with a pretty ribbon. They make a great hostess gift or impromptu present for neighbors and friends.

Superhero Status Organize your own work party as a way to give back to the community. Many parks or local organizations will be thrilled to have an organized group of five to fifteen people ready to get down and dirty! Perhaps it's a birthday or a special anniversary. Or it's "just because." Socialize, sweat, and save the earth, all at the same time!

Chapter 4
Winter

Sitting with Your Soul

"Winter is the time for comfort, for good food and warmth, for the touch of a friendly hand and for a talk beside the fire: it is the time for home."
—*Edith Sitwell*

Harsh weather comes in the form of wind, rain, snow, and ice, forcing all things to seek shelter and batten down the hatches. This weather also brings with it calm, quiet, and peace throughout the season. Winter is a time of outward inactivity, of bare branches and stagnant growth. However, underneath, the roots are being set to provide strength in preparation for the busy seasons to come.

It's the perfect time for us to quiet down and settle in as well. Like the earth, we are outwardly less active, but just underneath the surface our minds and souls are dynamic and working. We warm ourselves with cozy fires and companionship. It's a time to think new thoughts and dream new dreams.

In winter you will:

- Make time for soul connection.
- Channel your inner chef.
- Lighten and brighten your space.
- Play in the rain.

Living Your Intentions

Chieko Watanabe, Life Coach

"Your work is to discover your world and then with
all your heart give yourself to it."
—*Buddha*

As the days get shorter and winter sets in, I start to feel the call of hibernation. In the northern latitude of Seattle, it's dark when we wake up and go to work, and it's dark before the workday is done. I want nothing more than to curl up with a good book and a hot cup of tea.

Finding "You" Time

Winter is a natural time for us to quiet down and hibernate. Yet, with our busy lives it seems impossible to sit for more than 10 minutes without feeling guilty or like we should be doing something productive. We get so accustomed to the bustle of all the things we have to do, the people we need to see, the work that needs to get done, and the noise of social media and pop culture. We've forgotten how to be quiet. Our sense of self gets lost in the shuffle.

When we have guests at our house, Mr. Murphy, my cat, will duck into the back of my closet so as not to get caught underfoot and smushed by all the traffic and activity. It's really too bad, because he's a 21-pound cat. Quite the sight to see! But, no matter how much coaxing I do, he just won't come out. Within minutes after the last guest has said goodbye and the quiet settles back into the house, we hear the pitter-patter of his feet on the hardwood floors as he makes the trek from the bedroom into the living room. He'll give me a courtesy meow or two and then promptly sprawl his whale-like body on the floor.

Like Mr. Murphy, your soul may be tucked away, waiting for the environment to settle down and feel safe before venturing out. Our souls need quiet and time in order to reappear in full glory and stretch out before us.

The Getaway

My favorite way to find delicious soul-connecting time is to get some distance . . . literally. There's something about getting physically away from all the to-dos and errands that calms the mind and gives you a new perspective from which to view your life. Once the quiet of the environment settles into your body, mind, and spirit, you'll fully unplug from the constant stream of busyness. Now your real self can finally show up.

Every winter, I take time to escape the distractions of my home and office and sneak away to a cozy cabin in the woods where it's snowy, quiet, and magical. I pack nothing more than some warm clothes, a few toiletries, groceries for some home-cooked meals, a good book, and my journal. Yes, I admit, I bring my phone (mostly because it's my watch, camera, music player, and alarm clock), but my intention for the trip is to literally and figuratively get some distance from my life. It's my quiet time to be alone with my thoughts and reflect.

If it's your first time for a quiet getaway, it may take a day or two

A Note on Feelers and Feelers

It's easy to confuse feelings for your feelers. Feelings are emotions, such as hurt, sadness, delight, joy, and so on.

We experience these feelings with our feelers. Just like great music that wants to be heard, and beautiful art that wants to be seen, feelings just want to be felt. When you take the time to use your feelers, the feeling can be experienced and then move on, and you can finally be free. You don't have to take feelings personally— they are just passing through.

to fully shift gears to quiet mode. Often what bubbles up is the sadness or pain that we've buried with all the busyness. Perhaps it's feelings of loneliness, the fear of facing the truth about something you've been putting off, or the realization that you've been living off-purpose. Whatever you've been pushing down, it's time to let it come up.

Ahhhh, now it's quiet—really quiet. Our environment and all those feelings are quiet, too. Now we can take an honest look at our lives and see what's going amazingly well, and what could change for the better. Only from this haven of quiet and solitude can you reflect from an intuitive, soulful place rather than from societal expectations or other people's opinions.

A Little Soul Chat

So what do you do with all this quiet time? It's a great place to give voice to your heart and your soul. Here's a little guide to help you get started:

1. Ask your heart, what does she really want? Brainstorm and jot down all the things that come up. Even if they seem selfish or overindulgent, don't judge them. Let the ideas be heard.

2. Ask your soul, how does she want to BE? Does she want you to be braver, more focused, more grounded? Brainstorm and jot down everything you hear.

3. What would it mean to you if you had all these things you wanted and were being the person your soul wanted? How would your life be different?

Intention

Take a look at the messages you have received and set some intentions for yourself. Intentions are different from goals—they serve as your commitment. Intentions, like vows, are promises you make to yourself that act as guideposts from which to navigate. It's important to have goals; however, you must stay connected to the original intention behind the goal.

For example, you might set a goal to call your mother once a week, or do something nice for your spouse every day. However, you must stay connected to the original intention behind the goal so your mother and spouse don't just become to-do items being checked off your list (and they don't want that either).

In my intentions, I have always found answers to where I've wandered off course, no matter how obscure or challenging the problem. When I reconnect with my intention, it becomes clear what I need to do. For example, whenever my partner and I find ourselves in a real relationship quandary, I turn to the intention I set for our relationship. There, I find my contribution to the problem, as well as my solution. Here's an example of the intention I have for my relationship with my partner:

To be open and honest; to trust and love freely; to be supportive and compassionate; to consistently express appreciation and gratitude; to show kindness and affection; to take care of myself in all areas of my life so I can be the best lover, friend, and partner that I can be; to have the courage to ask for what I need and desire; to be open to receive love and support in return; to resolve any issues quickly and learn from them; to forgive our mistakes and let them go; to love you just as you are, for everything you are.

When my partner or I have screwed up and I'm struggling with it, I look to my intentions and am reminded that I need to *"forgive our mistakes and let them go."* When my partner gets swamped and I'm feeling disconnected, I know I need to *"have the courage to ask for what I need"* and request some attention.

I Need Attention

We all need attention sometimes, and in the absence of positive attention, we'll go so far as to seek negative attention. I've learned that it's really vital for our happiness to be able to ask for attention, especially from our partners, to avoid the buildup of resentment. Too often it leads to passive-aggressive behavior that slowly poisons the relationship.

Next time you feel a bit neglected, insignificant, or lonely, rather than expecting your partner to read your mind and anticipate your every need, try asking for attention. I do this by making my sad face, lightly touching my partner, and saying, "I need attention . . ." I do it with a touch of humor, but I'm asking for something I really need.

In addition to your intentions, it's great to set goals for yourself. A goal takes these intentions you've set and turns them into action. Goals help you laser your focus to reach the next milestone.

In the case of my relationship, I've set the intention to *"forgive our mistakes and let them go."* I'll admit that forgiveness has never been my forte. So the goal I set for myself is to practice *ho'oponopono* when I'm holding on to anger, until I feel the full release.

Ho'oponopono is a traditional Hawaiian practice of forgiveness. What I love about *ho'oponopono* is that it's a simple yet powerful tool to let go of any anger you may be holding against yourself or someone else and invite peace into your heart.

How to Ho'oponopono

Start by taking a breath and filling your heart with love and compassion. Bring to mind the person you felt hurt by and you'd like to forgive. Then say the ho'oponopono mantra:

I love you.
I'm sorry.
Please forgive me.
Thank you.

Say these statements again and again until you start to feel a shift and a release in your heart. Breathe and let the energy of forgiveness flow in and exhale the negativity out. Continue to fill your heart with the energy of love and compassion.

Forgiveness can be a process. When I feel really hurt, it's difficult for me even to say these words. But with a few repetitions I can feel the loosening of the grip those feelings have over me, creating space for compassion and peace.

A Final Note on Magic

Winter is a time of magic. It's a time for delight, enchantment, and love. By setting your intentions and goals, you illuminate the pathway with inviting, twinkling lights for the magic of the universe to find it's way to you. It's when you meet the exact person you needed to meet, when the perfect opportunity practically falls in your lap, when you begin to see the world in a whole new way, that you'll know the universe has found its way to your open door. When our goals support our intentions, that's when the magic happens.

Action Plan

Schedule You Time Block some time on your calendar for some "you" time and have a Little Soul Chat. Don't forget to bring your favorite notebook.

Write Your Intentions In your notebook, write intentions for yourself for the different areas of your life. Remember, these are your written commitments and will help guide you going forward.

Channeling Your Inner Chef
Michelle Babb, MS, RD, Nutritionist

"This is my invariable advice to people: Learn how to cook- try new
recipes, learn from your mistakes, be fearless, and above all have fun!"
—*Julia Child*, My Life in France

The winter season perfectly highlights our body's natural tendency
to be in sync with nature. My clients report a desire to slow down, stay
inside, do more cooking, and eat heartier, starchier foods. This is a tes-
tament to biological programming that dates back to Paleolithic times
or perhaps even earlier. When food is less plentiful, we have a natural
tendency to want to conserve energy by sleeping more, moving less, and
eating foods that are warming and satiating.

Right about now you're probably rejoicing that a dietitian has given
you permission to lounge about and eat comfort foods all winter long
but, alas, I have a slightly different take on our modern adaptation to
winter. While I think it makes sense (in most parts of the country) to
eat mostly what's in season, our need to stockpile calories and be stingy
with our energy has greatly diminished. Gone are the days of the traditional hunter-gatherer. We hunt for our meat from the deli counter at
the supermarket. We gather our fresh food from the beautiful displays
in the produce section, promptly rejecting slightly bruised apples and
less-than-perfect potatoes. We really have to make an effort to strike a

balance between honoring our evolutionary tendencies and acknowledging that modern conveniences have forever altered the playing field.

Crying Out for Kale

In the spirit of full disclosure, I will tell you that I'm crazy for kale. I'm in awe of its nutritional properties, and I love that you can eat it raw, sautéed, steamed, boiled, or baked. It also happens to be the perfect example of a sturdy plant that can survive the mild winters of the Pacific Northwest and be a great source of nourishment when you need it most. It's packed with B vitamins and antioxidants and is great for the immune system.

With all that said, I have relatives and friends who are actually astonished that anyone would willingly eat the curly greens that are so often used to garnish a fruit or vegetable platter. Preconceived notions about less familiar foods often prevent us from enjoying the culinary delicacies that nature has to offer. This is why I urge people to use that natural nesting tendency we have in the colder months to be adventurous in the kitchen and experiment with unfamiliar foods. I had never tried kale, Brussels sprouts, or fresh beets until I was in my late twenties, and now they're among my favorite foods.

Pocket Full of Beets

A client once told me she had a traumatic experience with beets as a child. She was at her grandmother's house and had been served canned beets and was told to clean her plate before getting up to play. When Grandma wasn't looking, she cleverly stuffed the beets into the pockets of her jacket that was hanging on the back of her chair. By the time she got home, though, the beet juice had leaked through both coat pockets of her light-colored jacket. Her mother nearly had a heart attack, thinking that her daughter had some inexplicable injury! Needless to say, beets weren't high on my client's list of culinary must-haves.

We all have one of those pocket-full-of-beets-type stories that leaves an indelible mark. Perhaps it keeps us from trying or enjoying certain foods in adulthood. If your only experience with cauliflower is eating the inhumanely overcooked steam-table version, PLEASE try it roasted, mashed or thinly sliced and sautéed. In fact, if there are any vegetables that you've only tried steamed, get creative with your cooking methods and give them another chance.

Five Ways to Fall in Love with Beets

1. Shred them raw into a salad (skins and all!).
2. Roast them by tossing them with grapeseed oil, adding salt, and baking at 425°F until tender.
3. Steam them, remove the skins, and toss with olive oil and balsamic vinegar.
4. Pickle them.
5. Juice them.

Examine Your Family Food Culture

As you uncover your own pocket-full-of-beets memories, you may get some much-needed insight into certain eating habits you've formed over the years. Many of my clients who claim to be emotional eaters have distinct memories of food as love or food being used as a reward. If you've ever said to yourself, "I'm going to eat this whole pan of brownies because I had a hard week and I DESERVE IT!" then you may be a food-as-reward victim. If you're constantly making delectable baked goods for your spouse, kids, and coworkers, you may have a firmly held belief that food equals love. Awareness of the root cause of these behaviors may help you eliminate unwanted habits.

I often ask clients to do a genogram, which is similar to a family tree, to illustrate the relationship that different generations of family members have with food and eating. I tell them that a healthy relationship with food is defined as eating nourishing foods to satisfy physical hunger. Rarely do I find a long lineage of family members who have a perfectly healthy relationship with food. Just the opposite is true. Most of my clients notice that they've never had a good example of what it looks like to enjoy food in a non-abusive, healthy way. Many realize that they are repeating those patterns and passing unwelcome habits on to the next generation.

Take a good, close look at your current food culture. Does it support your vision of wellness? If you have a family, do you see healthy food habits being cultivated within your family? If you're single and live alone, are you satisfied with how you are choosing to nourish yourself? If the answer to these questions is a resounding "NO," then spend some time thinking about what needs to change to create a supportive food culture in your home.

You can do a pantry makeover to throw out all the junk and make room for the good stuff. You can recruit family members to help with meal planning and prep work so that fresh food is abundant and ready to eat. It's okay to start small. Remember that you're trying to shift beliefs and patterns that have been in place for decades, so be patient and reward yourself for small successes (but not with food).

Food Bullies and Seasonal Sabotage

It would be difficult, if not impossible, to examine your family food culture without making some observations about the holiday season. For many of us, holiday celebrations center around food, and we give ourselves express permission to eat with reckless abandon. Why not? It's the holidays, after all. It's time to eat, drink, and be merry. As we all know, mindless holiday eating is certainly not without consequence. Many of the clients I see in January and February come in complaining that they were derailed during the holidays and are filled with regret, shame, hopelessness, and sometimes anger.

I have a client, we'll call her Dana, who has a long history of allowing herself to be bullied into eating poorly. Friends would insist she share heaping plates of nachos or fried mozzarella sticks. They would poke fun at her attempts to resist, questioning how long she would stay on her latest health kick. We spent many sessions discussing the importance of speaking up for herself and not betraying her desire to eat healthy. She was making great progress until she scheduled a trip home for the holidays. Just planning the trip evoked some strong emotions and illuminated a lifelong pattern of being agreeable in order to keep the peace.

"I just don't think I'll be able to stay on my nutrition plan while I'm at home," explained Dana. She said that her mom had always been in complete control of all meals and anything related to food. In fact, Dana was not even allowed to be in the kitchen when her mom was preparing meals. "It's just easier to go along with it because I don't want to get into a war with my mom," said Dana. While I can appreciate the desire to avoid conflict with family, particularly around the holidays, I asked her to think about the bigger issue. Her tendency to always put everyone else's thoughts, desires, and behaviors toward food in front of her own was self-sabotaging. I challenged her to find a way to be true to her intention and eat foods that are congruent with her wellness vision.

Dana left my office in doubt that she would have the courage to stand up to her mom. When she came back a few weeks later, she was proud to report that she had made it a point to stick with her nutrition plan. She packed healthy snacks and even had a productive conversation with her mom about the positive changes that she noticed as a result of eating better, but not dieting. "The conversation wasn't nearly as bad as I had anticipated," said Dana. "I guess I just made it into a much bigger deal in my head and that was the story I was telling myself."

Dana's situation is not uncommon. When you're actively making changes to live a healthier lifestyle, there will be people in your life who are less than supportive and may even be guilty of sabotage. Usually it's related to their own guilt or fear that your positive changes somehow amplify their negative choices. Nothing makes this more evident than when you have friends or family members who use the holidays as an excuse for chronic overindulgence and they rely on you to be their partner in crime. When you resist and honor your right to make better choices, it causes discordance and is downright uncomfortable for everyone involved. The more you demonstrate consistency in your choices, the less others will feel compelled to bring you to the dark side.

This is one of my favorite quotes from another client, who happens to be one of the most inspirational women I've had the pleasure of meeting. At age 70 she decided it was high time to start eating foods that would improve her quality of life.

"I'm learning how to practice what's right for me . . . mindful eating.

Playful and nourishing and healing. I now have the energy to gently speak up for myself at guest tables without judgment of others and their preferences. I often ate food I would never eat at home and then hate myself for hours afterward. How self- demeaning is that for me, a woman who has long admired women who speak up for themselves? I feel lighter and better because I'm deepening my commitment to cherish myself, physically and spiritually."

Schlep It and Prep It

Recently a journalist asked me how I stay healthy during the holiday season. I explained that I use the same planning and food prep strategies that keep me on track the rest of the year. The simple truth is that eating healthy doesn't just happen, unless you can afford to hire a personal chef and have meals magically appear. A little bit of planning and prep can go a long way.

Sunday is my designated grocery shopping day. I don't love to grocery shop, so I do it first thing in the morning, when I can sip on a latte and wander through the store at my own pace without fighting the crowds. When I get home from the store, I unpack the groceries onto the counter and make a deal with myself that nothing will go into the refrigerator without being washed, chopped, or prepped to make it more edible. I also cook up a few simple staples, like quinoa or brown rice, so that I have some whole grains that are ready to eat. When fresh food is ready to eat and waiting for you in the refrigerator, you'll be surprised at how much more fresh produce you and your family will eat.

Karen (our professional organizer) came up with a great idea that

> ## Food Prep for Success
>
> Dedicate time to planning, shopping, and food prep and put it on your calendar each week.
>
> - Wash and chop fresh produce so it's ready to eat.
> - Make a big salad.
> - Boil some eggs.
> - Make some brown rice or quinoa.
> - Bake or grill some chicken.

has vastly increased the amount of fresh fruits and vegetables her family eats. She tossed out the pullout produce bins in her refrigerator (where forgotten food would tend to rot). She replaced the bins with two of the old-school Tupperware sectioned serving trays. She filled one with chopped veggies (carrots, celery, radishes, cucumbers, and peppers) and even put some olives in the center. She filled the other with strawberries, blueberries, grapes, and chopped melons. Karen can't get over the reduction in waste and, more important, the fact that her kids are choosing to snack on fresh fruits and vegetables. Leave it to an organizer to come up with that brilliant system!

Action Plan

Let experimentation be the theme. Schedule time for menu planning, shopping, and food prep. Experiment with fresh foods that are unfamiliar.

- Make a grocery shopping date with yourself once a week and put it on your calendar.
- Use the prep list in the sidebar to set yourself up for success throughout the week.

- Challenge yourself with an unfamiliar veggie, fruit, legume, or whole grain once every couple of weeks to expand your food repertoire.

Filtering and Freshening Up

Karen Pfeiffer Bush, Professional Organizer

"There are two ways of spreading light; to be the candle
or the mirror that reflects it."
—*Edith Wharton*

If months were assigned specific colors, the winter months would be a rainbow of green, red, burgundy, gold, white, and red again. It's not the natural red-orange-yellow-green-blue-indigo-violet rainbow. In my mind, December is the color hog representing more than half of the winter rainbow—the heavy colors of green, red, burgundy, and gold. January quickly flips to white—shimmery, silver white. February is heart red. Of course, these color associations are the product of years of holiday brainwashing. In fact, there is an emotional association with these colors that is apparent in our lives and homes.

Understandably, we associate winter with dark and cold even though, historically, many cultures around the world celebrate festivals of light. This is because the winter solstice, December 21 to 22, in the northern hemisphere is actually the beginning of "longer" days, even though it may not feel like it for quite some time.

For centuries, people have celebrated the winter solstice with fires and candles, holiday lights and ceremonies, culminating with people oohing and aahing over festive illumination. The European tradition of lighting a Yule log at Christmas originated with the Scandinavian feast of Juul, which dates to pre-Christian times. On the December solstice, fires were lit to symbolize the heat, light, and life-giving properties of the returning sun. A Yule or Juul log was burned on the hearth. A piece of the log was kept as a good luck token to be used as kindling for next year's fire.

Lighten Up

Despite wonderful holiday lights, December in Seattle is dark, dark, dark. The sun sets at around 4 p.m. and our houses are, well, dark. As you deck your halls and plan for family meals and celebrations, a simple thing you can do to combat the dark is to evaluate your lighting. This may be as simple as replacing or wiping clean light bulbs. Dirty light bulbs can give off 20 percent less light. Over years of helping people prepare their homes for the real estate market, I'm always amazed at what a difference fresh, clean light bulbs and fixtures make.

Add task lighting to frequently used areas. A simple desk lamp can make a world of difference. For those who feel a little blue in the dark days of winter, consider adding a light therapy lamp to your work and/or relaxation area. In the northern regions, lack of natural light can have a serious effect on our mood and energy level. You can brighten your attitude and your

Cleaning Lights and Shades

- To clean lampshades made of paper, fabric, or fine silk, use a lamb's wool duster instead of a rag. For very dirty shades, use the brush attachment of your vacuum.
- Clean glass shades in a plastic tub filled with soapy water. Rinse thoroughly and dry well.
- To clean bulbs, wait until they are cool and wipe thoroughly with a damp cloth.
- Clean recessed can lights with a damp cloth.

space by improving the quality of light, whether it is therapeutic or just typical household lighting.

Out with the Elves, in with the New

January—shimmery, silver white January. I love the rich colors of December, but ahh . . . the relief of the white of January. I proudly wear the crown of Mrs. Christmas Jr. (my mom being the original Mrs. Christmas). I have every inch of my house decked and decorated with the December rainbow, and I love it. Come the day after Christmas, however, I'M DONE. I yearn for the clean, clear slate of January.

> ### Streak-Free Windows
> 1. Wash one side of a window with horizontal strokes and the other side with vertical strokes so you can pinpoint which side has a streak.
> 2. Wash your windows on a cloudy day because direct sunlight dries cleaning solutions before you can polish the glass properly.
> 3. Use crumpled newspaper instead of paper towels.
> 4. Wash windows from the top to the bottom to prevent drips.
> 5. Use a soft toothbrush or cotton swab to clean corners.

This year, we were in full swing in December and didn't miss a celebration or tradition. When we returned home after family celebrations all over the county, my first reaction upon opening the door to our house was fear. For a second, I thought our house had been ransacked. Christmas had thrown up in my living room. A band of elves had gone berserk.

December 26, alas, a time to wrap up the festival of chaos: the glorious, red, green, burgundy, gold chaos. Bring on the white of January!

In Japan, there is an end-of-year custom called *oosoji*. In contrast to the spring-cleaning common in the United States, *oosoji* is traditionally practiced when the weather is cold. Many Japanese welcome the New Year with a clean slate by clearing and organizing at home, work, and school before the New Year's holiday.

If you are fully motivated to undertake an extensive *oosoji* at home, then by all means you should go for it and send me before and after pictures, PLEASE. However, if your colorful December zapped your energy, a great way to bring it back is by refreshing your space in smaller ways:

- Wash your windows, at least on the inside, if Mother Nature isn't cooperating for you to do the outside too. Let whatever light there is shine in.
- If it's not blowing, raining, or snowing sideways, turn off your heat for a couple of hours and open your windows. Let in some fresh air.
- Add a few houseplants to naturally filter the air.

You may find that you have an increase in energy and can think more clearly with less visual stimulus in your space. Lighten up your décor. Add a white or neutral-colored duvet to your winter comforter. Put white towels in your bathroom. Reduce the artwork and accessories on your mantle, side tables, and shelves. See how it feels to be lighter for a bit.

February is the heart of winter. Although it's cliché, I can't help but think of hearts and roses in February and, okay, chocolate too. Let's corny it up a notch and talk about the heart of your home and consider these questions:

- Where do you truly get comfy and spend the most quality time in your home?
- Think about the space that soothes your heart and soul.
- What is it about that space that warms you?
- Can those attributes be applied to other areas of your home or, perhaps more esoterically, to your life?
- Is your space filled with things that you love?
- Is it solitary or right smack in the middle of the action?

As you keep things as light as possible through the dark, colorful days of winter, embrace what makes your home cozy and bright. Focus on lightening and brightening the wonderful journey through the rainbow of winter. Your pot of gold awaits!

Action Plan

- **Lighten up:** Clean light fixtures, clean or replace light bulbs, add task lighting. Check flashlights and battery stores.
- **Freshen up:** Add whites and neutrals to your décor. Wash windows and air out your home.
- **Appreciate:** Make a list of the attributes of your comfiest spaces and see whether you can bring those attributes to other places in your home.

Puddle Jumping and Plant Snipping

Wendy Lomme, Landscape Designer

"I realize there's something incredibly honest about trees in winter,
how they're experts at letting things go."
—Jeffrey McDaniel

I was fortunate enough to grow up surrounded by several acres of trees in a semi-suburban town in Connecticut. I spent hours upon hours out in the woods exploring, playing with my siblings or friends, and tracking my cats to see what they did with their days. In the winter, we would ice skate on the pond and turn the hilly trails into sledding race tracks, including jumps and wipeout zones, of course! One of my favorite activities, though, was to listen to the snow fall. So calm. So serene. So magical. The hush that comes over the woods is breathtaking. I imagine the earth resting, finally taking time for itself to just be.

Make Like a Tree

Winter is a very introspective time, mainly because the weather encourages it. With freezing temperatures, chilling winds, and shorter days, the shelter our home provides is welcome and needed. While you are curled up safely on your couch, your mind and body are at rest and peaceful. The introspection comes on slowly. Just like the trees, you are settling in for the winter.

Grandma and the Stolen Starts

My mom told me that my grandmother used to carry scissors and a baggie around with her and snip anything that caught her eye. Truth be told, she would do this at nurseries as well as public spots. We all have skeletons (or stolen plants) in our closet, right? My grandma would sprout the stolen starts in cups of water placed on a large copper tray filled with pebbles. I have a few cups around my house, too, albeit from plants I already own, but I'm happy to be carrying on the tradition!

Take the vine maple, for example. After the brilliant fall color display of vibrant oranges and yellows, the leaves are shed, as they are no longer needed to absorb sunlight and produce food for the tree. While the branches are bare and resting, though, there is plenty going on under the ground. The roots are still growing, taking advantage of the warm-enough soil and abundant water.

We seem to mimic the trees: calm and quiet on the outside, but our minds are active on the inside. We review the past year coming to a close, and summarize the ups and downs, highs and lows. We take time to think of the year ahead, and start planning and dreaming. When we embrace this period of introspection, our roots will grow strong and we'll be ready to really shine come spring and summer.

I love that the winter weather encourages us to cozy up on the couch. But there's also ample opportunity to connect with nature during the winter. We don't see a ton of snow in the area where I live, but we do get plenty of the other wet stuff—rain! There's a certain mind-set that's necessary for being out in the rain. I find that I dread going out in it, but once I'm in it, I actually like it. Rain can be persistent, overwhelming, and irritating . . . but if you let go and succumb to the rain, it can be peaceful, melodic, and almost trance-like. For me, it pushes all other thoughts out of my mind. I find myself focusing on the task at hand, whether it is walking my dogs, running, or doing yard work. Being out in the rain also gives me a sense of rebellion. Is a little wet and cold going to keep me inside? Here's your guide to showing the rain what's up.

Rockin' Rain Rebellion!

Feet: Rain boots are a MUST! With my knee-high boots, do you think I avoid puddles? NO WAY!

Body: Layering is important to every winter activity—thermals, vest, gloves, etc. Also, contrary to popular belief, rain doesn't usually fall down as much as it does at an angle. With that in mind, keep your legs protected, either with rain pants (heck, you can roll in the grass if you want to) or a longer raincoat.

Face: If you're walking or running with any formidable speed, there's nothing worse than squinting because the stupid rain keeps spitting in your face. Your answer: a hat with a brim, either waterproof or to wear under your hood.

Mind: Hear the rebel yell! Go jump in some puddles! Walk through the mud and listen to the awesome noises. Go really *crazy* and plant your butt on the ground or on a bench, and just . . . sit. Just sit and listen.

Understanding that we all can't frolic in the rain every day, find other ways to enjoy the outdoors during the seemingly dreary and boring winter. Here are some ideas:

- **Bring the winter inside.** My mom never leaves home without her pruners. Yes, she is that crazy lady who will pull over on the side of the road to take a snip of a cool-looking plant. Now, I'm not condoning wandering the streets and lopping down your neighbor's dogwood tree. Perhaps start in your own yard, and see what you find. There are several plants that have berries this time of year (holly, cotoneaster, snowberry). There are tons of plants with cool branches (curly willow, dogwood, strawberry tree). Add some filler with snippets of evergreens (laurel, fir, camellia) and sprigs of ornamental grasses.
- **Feed the birds.** Speaking of berries, the birds are definitely taking advantage of this midwinter feast. Attract some excitement in your yard with a bird feeder, placed strategically so you can admire it from the cozy indoors.
- **Star light, star bright.** Maybe not, considering the abundant clouds and rain. So, bring some celestial light into your yard. Uplighting is not used nearly as much as it should be, in my opinion. If you have a favorite tree or large shrub, consider installing uplights to create a focal point and add depth to your yard. To easily add some sparkle, put lanterns or large outdoor lights in your favorite tree.
- **Use your windows.** Make sure you have at least one comfy lookout spot to admire your cool plants, the birds, and the pretty lights. To create some inspiration, replace a few downspouts on your house

and/or garage with rain chains. They create little splashes of water, and it's an added bonus if you can hear them through the window.

Action Plan

- Purchase or delegate a pair of "to-go" pruners to take in your car or on walks.
- Gear up and get outside. Go play in the rain!
- Create your cozy window perch to admire the great outdoors.
- Come up with some indoor family traditions you can honor and carry on, such as canning, growing orchids, or drying herbs.

Conclusion

We laughed. We cried. We pondered. We danced. But most of all, we wrote from our hearts to share with you our expertise and our personal stories in hopes that our message leads you to be light hearted, self-forgiving, and in regular celebration of your authentic self – flying pigs and all.

For more great information, visit us at our websites!
www.chiekowatanabe.com
www.eatplaybe.com
www.lifespaceseattle.com
www.akinadesigns.com

Acknowledgments

Chieko

My deepest gratitude to my life partner, John Frank, for your endless love and support. Thank you for your encouragement, for always being willing to drive me to and fro from our writing meetings, and for being a willing Guinea pig to my many life improvement ideas. You inspire me everyday.

A huge thank you to my partners-in-crime, Michelle, Karen, and Wendy, for bravely sharing your hearts, stories, expertise and homes to bring our vision to life. It has been such an honor to work with brilliant, loving, gorgeous human beings such as yourselves. This journey is one I will remember and cherish for the rest of my days.

Last but not least, a shout out to my favorite wineries and wines: Dunham Cellars for the amazing Three Legged Red, Palouse Winery for the very special Black Pearl Petite Sirah, and Cave B for the memorable Cuvee du Soleil. Such delightful companions to our creative process in writing this book.

Michelle

From the moment we shared that first bottle of wine at a local watering hole aptly called the Mission and said "we should write a book together," I knew I was in for an adventure of a lifetime. I will be forever grateful to my fellow Quillettes (Chieko, Karen, and Wendy) for inspiring me to put pen to paper and showing me that it IS possible for four women to happily collaborate on a project and still emerge as friends. As Ernest Hemmingway once said, "It is good to have an end to journey toward; but it is the journey that matters, in the end." And this has been one hell of a journey!

A debt of gratitude also goes to my loving husband, Bill Babb, who sometimes wondered if we were actually writing a book or having a series of wine tasting parties but was supportive nonetheless.

A big thank you to all of my clients who let me into their lives and inspire and amaze me. I am deeply grateful to have a job that teaches me something new about how extraordinary human nature is every single day.

And finally, many thanks to the suppliers of the juice that fueled our creativity: àMaurice's Viognier, Kerloo Cellars for making us all fans of Tempranillo, and Bin 41 for introducing us to those delightful little bottles of champagne. The celebration is never ending!

Karen

To my wonderful sons, Miles and August, a constant source of love and entertainment: thank you for allowing me to experiment on you. I must say, you're turning out pretty darn well!

To my husband, Jeb, my rock: good job holding down the fort over the many months of writing evenings and weekends. Thank you for always encouraging me to pursue my dreams even though you're sometimes shaking your head while you do it. I love you!

To my writing partners: I will be forever grateful for sharing this fun and crazy ride with you brilliant, hilarious women. And to think.....this is just the beginning.

Thank you to all of the many waiters, waitresses, bartenders and fellow customers who have inquired what we were writing ...and laughing about. Cheers to you!

Thank you to Bin 41 and Chateau St. Michelle for helping to keep it all light.

Last but not least, thank you to Dr. Patrick Hunter for fixing my back after the writing session-turned-dance-party injury! That's a story for a different book!

Wendy

In memory of my Aunt Donna, a lifelong teacher in the classroom and out. She helped to inspire my focus in college and drive as a student, starting with allowing me to correct her student's papers when I was a young pup. I am so fortunate to have not only her, but my mom, sister and Aunt Betty as role models of intelligent, strong, capable women.

Acknowledgments

My co-authors are an inspiration to me, and I greatly appreciate their advice about business, life, love, and every other topic we've covered over hundreds of hours together. They are my mentors, sisters and lifelong friends.

Thank you to the many establishments in Seattle who put up with our "meetings". We managed to garner a few fans of the book before we were even done writing. Laughter is contagious!

18085212R00081